-7 II
09- 06'2 - 15

BRITAIN'S LAST
MUNICIPAL OPERATORS

BRITAIN'S LAST
MUNICIPAL OPERATORS

Gavin Booth

Ian Allan
PUBLISHING

First published 2012

ISBN 978 0 7110 3547 8

Published by Ian Allan Publishing –
an imprint of Ian Allan Publishing Ltd, Hersham,
Surrey, KT12 4RG.
Printed in China.

Visit the Ian Allan Publishing website at
www.ianallanpublishing.com
Distributed in the United States of America and Canada
by BookMasters Distribution Services.

FRONT COVER: Lothian Buses – See page 100.

BACK COVER (UPPER): Reading Buses has also used colours
to distinguish its principal corridors. This is a 2011 Alexander
Dennis Enviro400H diesel-electric hybrid for the Purple 17 route.
Mark Lyons

BACK COVER (LOWER): Cardiff Bus has applied a range of
strongly-branded liveries to its busiest routes, as on this
2007 Scania OmniCity. Mark Lyons

PREVIOUS PAGE Several of the remaining municipal bus
companies have gone for colour-coded route-branded buses
or have brightened their previously traditional liveries. In 2012
Ipswich Buses adopted this bold scheme, worn here by a 2002
East Lancs Lowlander-bodied DAF DB250. Mark Lyons

ABOVE Some of the remaining municipal bus companies have
adopted colour-coding for their branded services. In this specially
posed shot, buses representing most of Reading's 2012 brands
are lined up in all their glory. Mark Lyons

Contents

Introduction

The first sight of an Edinburgh Corporation bus was always a reassuring and comforting one as we returned from family holidays when I was younger. I imagine other bus enthusiasts lucky enough to live in towns and cities served by municipal buses might have experienced similar feelings. Today, more than 35 years since local-government reorganisation changed Edinburgh Corporation buses into Lothian Region buses, I still experience that *frisson* when I catch sight of a Lothian bus as I return home.

I am lucky that I live in a city where the majority of the local bus services are provided by a council-owned bus fleet. A century ago there were few towns and cities of any size in the UK that did not have municipally owned tramcars; at one time there were

well over 100 corporation-owned fleets, and even 50 years ago there were still more than 90.

In the early years of the last century it became a matter of municipal pride to walk down urban streets populated by busy electric tramcars, each one proudly bearing the corporation's crest and often the name of the undertaking in bold gilt-edged, probably shaded letters. It was a sign that this was a town that kept up with the latest fashions and was spreading outwards to provide housing for people who worked there but wanted to live in more attractive surroundings. Municipal trams did much to encourage the growth of the suburbs, allowing people who had previously needed to live within walking distance of their workplace to commute quickly and cheaply to work.

ABOVE Reading Buses was an early user of the latest generation of diesel-electric hybrid buses. This 2011 Alexander Dennis Enviro400H 78-seater displays 'Claret Routes' branding for services linking the centre of Reading with the university. Mark Lyons

Some town councils in Britain chose not to run their own local transport. Some were content to leave this to commercial companies, many of which had sprung up to develop and build the newfangled electric tramways. In terms of population in 1901 Bristol, Stoke-on-Trent, Norwich, Gateshead and York were the largest towns and cities that never operated their own electric tramways, while places like Cambridge and Oxford, which never did so for different reasons, still had relatively low populations at the start of the 20th century.

Not that population was always a factor. Looking at the towns that invested in electric trams, some had populations in six figures, and others were barely into five figures at the time. The trams undoubtedly helped some of these towns to flourish and grow, but it must have been a slightly anxious investment for some smaller town councils.

Although the cost of upgrading trams and track caused some municipal tramway undertakings to sell out to bus companies, the rest turned to motor buses and sometimes trolleybuses and at the same time some continued to invest heavily in their tram systems.

So the number of councils operating their own urban transport systems remained fairly stable until local-government reorganisations caused some changes in the 1960s and 1970s, notably the creation of the Passenger Transport Executives between 1969 and 1974, followed by a rash of sales in the 1990s, encouraged by the Government.

It is always dangerous to quote the number of municipal operators remaining at the time of writing because the numbers have continued to drop, and between writing this in mid-2012 and the publication of this book there could be more casualties. Certainly, at the time of writing the number stands at 11 – only just in double figures, whereas 50 years ago the total was nudging three figures. It would be a brave person

to predict how many might survive for, say, five years, as circumstances can change. For some councils their arm's-length bus company represents a substantial part of the family silver, and in straitened economic times – possibly following a change of local political control – the temptation to sell might become too great.

What is interesting to note is that the survivors include well-regarded companies that regularly win industry awards. Certainly, the senior managers are often those who enjoy the freedom to make decisions locally without the sometimes lengthy communication lines and corporate baggage that can be found in the larger groups.

Gavin Booth
Edinburgh
May 2012

ABOVE The names of many municipal operators changed at the time of local-government reorganisation in 1974. Widnes Corporation became Halton Transport, and the former name and livery are recalled on this 2002 East Lancs Myllennium-bodied Dennis Dart, seen on service in Liverpool. Mark Lyons

LEFT Cardiff Bus invested in lighter-weight Dennis Darts for many years but in 2007 switched to Scanias, including East Lancs Olympus-bodied double-deckers and integral OmniCity single-deckers like this 53-seat articulated version, branded for 'Capital City Red' services. Mark Lyons

Chapter One
MUNICIPAL PRIDE

ABOVE In 1967 the Hartlepool and West Hartlepool undertakings merged to form Hartlepool Corporation. Latterly Hartlepool ran ECW-bodied Bristol REs, like this 1970 RELL6L seen in 1980. Gavin Booth

Britain changed greatly during the 19th century. At the end of the 18th century the population had been mainly rural, but by the 1851 census most Britons lived in towns, usually as a consequence of the industrial revolution, which encouraged a mass migration of workers from poor rural areas to the fast-growing towns and cities in areas like the Midlands, north-west England and central Scotland. As the new railway network grew in the second half of the 19th century, towns grew up at junctions and wherever the railway companies established their head offices and workshops. By 1901, 77% of Britons lived in towns and cities, around 40% of them in London and the conurbations that 70 years later would merit their own passenger-transport authorities – Clydeside, Tyneside, West Yorkshire, south-east Lancashire, Merseyside and the West Midlands.

But there were also long-established cities that grew dramatically, like Norwich, Oxford and York, where in the course of the 19th century the population tripled (in the case of Norwich) or even quintupled (Oxford). And the growth was driven not only by the industrialisation of Britain but also by the growth of seaside resorts, as more workers used railways to reach these places on half-day and bank holidays.

Municipal boroughs were created in England and Wales, working through elected town councillors and paid officials. In Scotland municipal burghs worked in a similar way.

Good public transport became essential as towns and cities expanded, often to counteract the effects of cramped and insanitary housing close to factories and other industrial premises. Suburban living became a dream for many, and fast and cheap railway and tramway routes encouraged this.

At the end of the 19th century tramways were seen as the way forward. In many urban areas there had been horse-drawn tramways and often horse buses too, but modern, fast electric trams revolutionised local transport, and between 1892 and 1907 there was a rush to convert to electric trams; opened during this period were more than 70 municipal systems that would survive into the 1960s running motor buses, as well as many more municipal and company-run tramways that would be subsumed by giants like London Transport or would sell out to local territorial bus companies.

It became a matter of municipal pride if you had an electric tramway system, a sign that this was an important town. Legislation in force allowed the corporation to build the tramway, but operations had to be leased to a separate private company, normally for 21 years. At the end of this period municipalities were able to buy back the lease and operate directly.

Municipalities could own and run the new motor buses. Many dipped a toe into this new and unproven mode, and a few experimented with the new 'trackless trolleybuses', but the poor state of many urban roads made tram travel the most attractive option. As motor buses and trolleybuses and the roads they used all improved, some municipals started to question the cost of running trams. As first-generation electric trams became due for

ABOVE A contrast in liveries and bus design at Dundee, with a preserved Dundee Corporation 1951 Daimler CVD6 with 56-seat Croft body in fully lined green/white livery alongside a 1979 MCW Metrobus of Tayside Regional Council, which ran the local buses following local-government reorganisation in 1975. Gavin Booth

ABOVE The municipal fleets at Middlesbrough and Stockton, together with the Tees-side Railless Traction Board, combined as Teesside Municipal Transport in 1968, renamed at local-government reorganisation in 1974 as the transatlantic-sounding Cleveland Transit. This 1971 Daimler Fleetline/Northern Counties was photographed in 1980. Gavin Booth

replacement and track and overhead needed upgrading, the bus often seemed a more attractive alternative.

By the time World War 2 broke out in 1939 more than 150 tramway systems had been abandoned, many of them small company-owned systems, but there were a few municipal casualties. The vast majority of the abandoned tramways were replaced by motor buses, including the municipal systems at Aberdare, Accrington, Barrow-in-Furness, Birkenhead, Burnley Colne & Nelson, Burton-on-Trent, Chester, Colchester, Exeter, Great Yarmouth, Halifax, Haslingden, Kilmarnock Lancaster, Lincoln, Lowestoft, Luton, Lytham St Annes, Newport, Northampton, Preston, Rawtenstall, Rochdale, Southport, Stockton-on-Tees, Swindon, Wallasey, Warrington, West Bromwich and Wigan. Others were replaced by trolleybuses, including the Bournemouth, Darlington, Doncaster, Grimsby, Hartlepool and West Hartlepool, Ipswich, Keighley, Pontypridd, Portsmouth, St Helens, Walsall and Wolverhampton systems, while a combination of buses and trolleybuses replaced the trams at Ashton-under-Lyne, Brighton, Chesterfield, Cleethorpes, Derby, Maidstone, Nottingham and Reading. Others were bought by the local company bus operator.

The corporation tramway systems at Coventry and Southend-on-Sea were replaced by motor buses during the war, and the Huddersfield system was replaced by

trolleybuses. In the five years after the war there was a rush of conversions from trams to motor buses (Blackburn, Bolton, Bury, Darwen, Leicester, Oldham, Plymouth, Rotherham, SHMD, Salford, and Southampton), or to motor buses and trolleybuses (Bradford, Cardiff, Hull, Manchester, Newcastle and South Shields).

This left a few of the major tramway systems, as well as some that had invested in new tramcars in the post-war years and some that were struggling on with elderly cars. Aberdeen, Birmingham, Dundee, Edinburgh, Leeds, Liverpool, Stockport and Sunderland all converted their tramway systems to motor-bus operation in the 1950s, while Belfast converted to motor buses and trolleybuses. This left just Blackpool, Glasgow and Sheffield running trams; the Sheffield system closed in 1960, and Glasgow's in 1962, but Blackpool famously kept going and in 2012 introduced 16 modern trams to upgrade its system, which had been running more or less continuously since 1885.

The number of municipal bus operators hovered around the 90 mark for most of the post-World War 2 years, with only the odd tweak, usually as a result of boundary and local-government changes.

Local-government changes in County Durham in 1967 resulted in the previously separate bus undertakings at Hartlepool and West Hartlepool merging to form Hartlepool County Borough Transport

ABOVE Teesside Municipal Transport buses wore this unusual turquoise/cream livery during the undertaking's short existence. This is a 1963 ex-Stockton Leyland Titan PD2/40 with 64-seat Metro-Cammell body.
Tony Wilson

Department. The two boroughs had worked together to operate trolleybuses, but when these were withdrawn in 1953 they went their separate ways, Hartlepool Corporation running a small fleet of buses through a local operator, and the larger West Hartlepool Corporation operating directly.

In 1968 the boroughs of Stockton-on-Tees and Middlesbrough and the urban district of Eston were merged as the county borough of Teesside, which meant that the former municipal bus fleets at Middlesbrough and Stockton and the Tees-side Railless Traction Board – a joint board formed by Eston and Middlesbrough that operated buses and trolleybuses – merged to form Teesside Municipal Transport, which had only a short existence under this name, as it passed to the new Cleveland county in 1974. Also in 1968 the corporation fleets at Haslingden and Rawtenstall merged to form Rossendale Joint Transport Committee. The same year saw West Bridgford UDC sell its bus undertaking to neighbouring Nottingham Transport.

The 91 municipal bus fleets that were operating in Britain at the start of 1969 were a substantial force. Their 18,000 buses represented more than one-third of the buses in the publicly owned sector, which at the time included London Transport, the National Bus Company and the Scottish Bus Group. Nine municipal buses in ten were double-deckers; there was just a handful of coaches and hardly anything that could be classed as a minibus or midibus, plus a mere 223 trolleybuses surviving in the Bournemouth, Bradford, Cardiff, Teesside and Walsall fleets – though these would all be gone by 1972.

But in 1969 the whole shape of urban transport was about to change, and so was the local influence that the municipal fleets had enjoyed.

Harold Wilson's Labour Government had came into power in 1964, and it soon became clear that charismatic transport minister Barbara Castle had an appetite for super-authorities planning and controlling transport in Britain's largest conurbations at least. She had been impressed by a 1966 visit to the United States and the San Francisco Bay Area Rapid Transit system. A 1966 White Paper laid the foundations in Britain for the creation of Conurbation Transport Authorities, later to emerge as Passenger Transport Authorities (PTAs) – policy-making bodies that controlled Passenger Transport Executives (PTEs). Initially it was unclear if this would mean that the municipal, company and independent operators in the PTA areas would be allowed to continue running their own buses under some form of centralised control, but with an increased majority in the 1966 general election Labour produced another White Paper, and this spelled out in detail the major changes that were coming.

RIGHT Looking slightly uncomfortable in West Midlands PTE colours, an ex-Wolverhampton Corporation Guy Arab V with 72-seat Metro-Cammell body in Sedgley in 1976. Tony Wilson

FACING PAGE ABOVE Manchester Corporation was by far the largest component of the new SELNEC PTE in 1969. In 1966, in Corporation days, two Daimler Fleetlines with 76-seat Metro-Cammell bodies, dating from 1963/4, stand in Manchester's Piccadilly bus station. Tony Wilson

FACING PAGE BELOW There was much label-sticking by PTEs until the buses of the former corporations could be repainted or replaced. This is an ex-Oldham Corporation 1957 Leyland Titan PD2/20 with 60-seat Roe body, pictured in 1974 in Oldham's final pommard/cream colours with SELNEC Southern logo covering the Oldham crest. Gavin Booth

The existence of the privately owned BET group had been a potential obstacle to Labour's grand plans, but its 1967 sale to the state-owned Transport Holding Company paved the way for the creation of the National Bus Company (NBC), which at the beginning of 1969 assumed control of more than 22,000 buses and coaches running in England and Wales. NBC was a formidable organisation, but right from the start some of its most lucrative bus services, operating in PTA areas, faced the threat of, at best, external control and, at worst, compulsory acquisition.

The first four PTEs, covering the West Midlands, Greater Manchester, Merseyside and Tyneside, started operating in 1969/70. Over the course of barely three months more than 6,000 municipal buses – roundly one-third – had been absorbed into the new PTEs. Twenty corporation undertakings – one fifth of the total at the start of 1969 – disappeared.

West Midlands PTE was dominated by Birmingham City Transport, which alone yielded more than 1,300 buses, and also took in the Walsall, West Bromwich and Wolverhampton fleets, with a further 678 vehicles between them, including Walsall's remaining 46 trolleybuses.

The Manchester area PTE was named SELNEC (South East Lancashire, North East Cheshire) and absorbed 11 municipal fleets, from mighty Manchester (1,222 buses) to tiny Ramsbottom UDC (12); the other constituents were Ashton, Bolton, Bury, Leigh, Oldham, Rochdale, SHMD (the Stalybridge, Hyde, Mossley & Dukinfield Transport & Electricity Board), Salford and Stockport.

Merseyside PTE had just three constituents – Liverpool (1,001 buses), Birkenhead (218) and Wallasey (73), providing a total fleet of 1,292. The River Mersey separated Liverpool from the other two fleets on the Wirral peninsula.

There was a much greater separation between the two fleets that made up the new Tyneside PTE – the physically separate Newcastle (341 buses) and South Shields (86) undertakings. Unlike the other PTEs, where the PTE bus fleets easily outnumbered those of NBC or independent operators, NBC companies operated more than 540 buses in the Tyneside area.

As we shall see, all four PTEs would grow as their areas expanded, and further PTEs would be created in the 1970s. And although it is really beyond the scope of this book, the first four PTEs expanded their influence over other operators in their areas in different ways, NBC selling the operations of two significant companies to the local PTEs – a substantial part of Midland Red to West Midlands, and the local North Western operations to SELNEC.

ABOVE The bright new SELNEC livery could look slightly anachronistic on traditional-looking double-deckers like this former Stockport Leyland Titan PD2/40 with 64-seat East Lancs body, seen in Manchester in 1973.
Gavin Booth

FACING PAGE ABOVE Birkenhead and Wallasey corporations formed Merseyside PTE's Wirral area. This 1964 Birkenhead Corporation Daimler Fleetline/Weymann 77-seater wears the undertaking's attractive blue/cream colours. Tony Wilson

FACING PAGE BELOW More label-sticking – in Liverpool in 1980, a former Liverpool Corporation Leyland Atlantean PDR1/1 with 71-seat Metro-Cammell body, with Merseyside PTE legal lettering and with the original MPTE logo added above the door. Gavin Booth

Chapter Two
EARLY CHANGES AND CASUALTIES

ABOVE Exeter Corporation sold its bus undertaking to the new National Bus Company in 1970. A former Exeter 1964 Leyland Titan PD2A/30 with 57-seat Massey body is seen in Devon General livery in 1979. Tony Wilson

The 70 municipalities that survived after the creation of the first PTEs could still muster more than 11,500 buses between them. With giants like Birmingham, Liverpool and Manchester out of the picture, the municipal fleets now ranged from Glasgow Corporation, with 1,242 buses, to tiny Welsh undertakings like Bedwas & Machen (seven buses) and Colwyn Bay (five).

But there were casualties. In 1970 Exeter Corporation sold its transport undertaking to the new National Bus Company, which merged it with the Devon General company, and in the same year Luton Corporation sold its bus operation to NBC's United Counties company.

But this situation was not to last for long. The success of the first four PTEs led to the creation of three more in the 1970s. The first, in 1973, was Greater Glasgow, absorbing the Glasgow Corporation fleet and covering an area much wider than that served by the municipal bus fleet. Next came South Yorkshire and West Yorkshire, which started up in 1974. The municipal undertakings that were merged to form South Yorkshire PTE were Sheffield (660 buses), Rotherham (124) and Doncaster (118), while West Yorkshire PTE was dominated by Leeds (686) but also absorbed the relatively sizeable Bradford (328), Halifax (223) and Huddersfield (219) fleets.

At the same time as the Yorkshire PTEs were starting up, the four original PTEs were expanded, accounting for the disappearance of five more municipal fleets. Merseyside grew with the addition of the St Helens (129 buses) and Southport (65) undertakings, SELNEC was renamed Greater Manchester and added 132-bus Wigan Corporation, Tyneside became Tyne & Wear, reflecting the absorption in 1973 of 166-bus Sunderland, while West

ABOVE Pictured in 1967, three years before Luton Corporation sold its buses to National Bus Company, a 1962 Leyland-Albion Lowlander LR7 with 65-seat East Lancs bodywork, with a lowbridge all-Leyland Titan PD2 behind. Tony Wilson

Midlands grew when it absorbed Coventry Corporation (329 buses). Thus in 1974 the PTEs claimed another 13 municipal undertakings, reducing the number of municipal buses by a further 4,421, to little more than 6,000.

But there were more changes as a result of local-government reorganisation in England and Wales in 1974. The old pattern with different tiers of local council – city, county borough, borough, urban district, rural district – gave way to new bodies, like metropolitan counties (in the big conurbation areas), borough councils and district councils. Long-familiar town and city names disappeared from the legal names of many local-authority fleets as undertakings adopted new names, sometimes where two or more were merged.

LEFT In 1975 the existing PTEs expanded as boundaries changed, and Southport Corporation's buses passed to Merseyside PTE. Seen in Southport in 1980, in MPTE colours but lacking fleetnames, is a 1973 ex-Southport Leyland Atlantean AN68/1R with 74-seat Alexander body. Gavin Booth

ABOVE In 1974 Wigan Corporation's buses passed to Greater Manchester (hitherto SELNEC) PTE. Pictured in Wigan in 1982 is an ex-Wigan Leyland Atlantean AN68/2R with locally built 79-seat Northern Counties bodywork in the latest brown/orange/white colours of GMPTE. Gavin Booth

Corporation name changes

New name (post-1974)	Previous name(s)
Aberconwy	Llandudno
Blackburn	Blackburn
	Darwen
Burnley & Pendle	Burnley, Colne & Nelson
Cleveland	Teesside
Colwyn	Colwyn Bay
Cynon Valley	Aberdare
East Staffordshire	Burton
Fylde	Lytham St Annes
Grampian	Aberdeen
Halton	Widnes
Hyndburn	Accrington
Islwyn	West Mon
Lancaster	Lancaster
	Morecambe & Heysham
Lothian	Edinburgh
Rhymney Valley	Bedwas & Machen
	Caerphilly
	Gelligaer
Taff-Ely	Pontypridd
Tayside	Dundee
Thamesdown	Swindon
Waveney	Lowestoft

The table shows the new names and the previous corporation names.

These changes reduced the total number of municipally owned bus fleets to just 50, as Darwen became part of Blackburn, Morecambe & Heysham was amalgamated with nearby Lancaster, and Bedwas & Machen, Caerphilly and Gelligaer were merged to form Rhymney Valley. Now Lothian Region Transport – the former Edinburgh Corporation undertaking – had the largest fleet, with over 600 buses, followed by Nottingham (370), Cleveland (282) and Kingston-upon-Hull (258).

The fleet composition was changing rapidly – a situation that was reflected in other parts of the bus industry. Whereas in 1969 nine out of ten municipal buses had been double-deckers, by 1980 this had fallen to seven out of ten as operators turned increasingly to high-capacity single-deckers that offered almost as many seats as a 56-seat double-decker and although in the early 1960s single-deckers had the advantage that they could be operated on a driver-only basis, saving the cost of conductors' wages, from 1966 double-deckers could also be operated with only a driver. Nonetheless, there were some significant converts to single-deck operation, among them Barrow, Blackpool, Colchester, Darlington, Great Yarmouth, Halton, Hartlepool,

Leicester, Lincoln, Maidstone, Newport, Northampton, Nottingham, Preston, Rossendale and Warrington.

The changes of name and local control led to new liveries as managers sought to shake off traditional municipal images and produce buses that were more eye-catching and contemporary. That was the theory, at least. The table below lists the municipalities that changed colour completely, either at the time of local-government reorganisation in 1974/5 or in the preceding five years; others applied their traditional colours in more contemporary ways. Others still adopted completely new liveries where two or more

municipal undertakings found themselves bundled into a new authority. Rhymney Valley, for example, was made up of Bedwas & Machen (blue), Caerphilly (green) and Gelligaer (red) and adopted a brown, yellow and cream livery; the new Lancaster undertaking adopted a blue livery, replacing Lancaster red and Morecambe & Heysham green. Many municipals simply changed the fleetnames, crests and legal lettering.

In little more than a decade the whole face of municipal transport in Britain had been changed almost beyond recognition. In 1960 it had looked as if the 97 municipal undertakings would continue to provide the majority of bus services in most of Britain's cities and larger towns. The biggest in 1960, in terms of fleet size, had been Birmingham City Transport, with more than 1,800 buses, but by 1970 this had been subsumed by the new West Midlands PTE, and the creation of the PTEs, followed by local-government reorganisation in the mid-1970s, reduced the number of municipalities to just 50; by the end of the decade there had been a further casualty, Waveney District Council, the former Lowestoft Corporation, having sold its transport undertaking to the local NBC subsidiary, Eastern Counties, in 1977.

The 1980s would see even greater upheaval in the British bus scene, as the regulation and ownership of bus operators came under Government scrutiny.

ABOVE Coventry Transport passed to West Midlands PTE control in 1974. In Coventry city centre in 1977 are two ex-Coventry Daimler Fleetlines – a 1968 ECW-bodied 72-seat example, still in Coventry red with WM logos, and a 1972 East Lancs-bodied 74-seater in full WMPTE livery. Gavin Booth

Livery changes

Operator	was	became
Brighton	red	blue
Cardiff	crimson	orange
Derby	green	blue
East Staffs (formerly Burton)	maroon	red/green
Islwyn (formerly West Mon)	maroon	blue
Merthyr Tydfil	red	orange
Tayside (formerly Dundee)	green	blue

FACING PAGE ABOVE From 1974 there were new municipal names to learn. This 1975 Leyland Leopard PSU3B/4R, with 52-seat East Lancs body new in 1983, displays the Hyndburn name that replaced Accrington. The bus had been acquired from Halton Transport in 1988. Tony Wilson

FACING PAGE BELOW Representing both a name change and the move to large-capacity rear-engined single-deckers is a Fylde Borough (formerly Lytham St Annes Corporation) 1972 Seddon RU with 47-seat Pennine bodywork, in St Annes in 1982. Gavin Booth

ABOVE In 1977 the Waveney (formerly Lowestoft) transport undertaking was sold to National Bus Company, to be absorbed into the Eastern Counties business. Here a 1951 Lowestoft Corporation AEC Regent III with 56-seat Massey body is seen in 1973 among a selection of contemporary motor cars. Tony Wilson

Chapter Three
THE BUSES
THEY RAN

ABOVE Traditional municipal fare in Northampton in 1973. For many years the Corporation bought Daimler CVG6s with Roe bodies; this is a 1963 example. Tony Wilson

Municipals tended to have very individual vehicle-buying policies, which often meant they operated interesting and sometimes quirky buses, in contrast to the big company fleets that bought increasingly standardised types as the 1970s and 1980s progressed and National Bus Company corporatism clicked in.

The trade magazine *Commercial Motor* used to produce invaluable biennial surveys of Britain's major bus fleets, and these provide an interesting picture of the composition of the municipal fleets, in terms of both chassis type and the split between double-deckers (once the municipal favourite) and the growing number of high-capacity single-deckers that joined fleets from the 1960s.

The December 1967 survey, the last before the creation of the first PTEs decimated their number, showed that the 94 municipal fleets operated a total of 17,821 motor buses – 16,425 double-deckers (92.17%) and 1,396 single-deckers (7.83%) – plus 340 double-deck trolleybuses. Leyland dominated the motor-bus figures (7,691, representing 43.4%), followed by Daimler (5,072, 28.6%), AEC (3,098, 17.5%) and Guy (1,327, 7.5%). No other chassis manufacturer's total even reached treble figures. Of the double-deckers just 20% were rear-engined, such types accounting for 22% of single-deckers.

There were 14 chassis types represented in the total municipal fleet in 1967, and even more bodybuilders. In practice only a handful of chassis manufacturers had the capacity to supply the needs of the largest operators, and in the postwar years the dominant manufacturers were AEC, Daimler, Guy and Leyland, which builders' products represented 98% of the total municipal fleet. Since 1962 AEC and Leyland had been under common ownership within the Leyland Motor Corporation, and Daimler and Guy were owned by Jaguar. In 1968 Leyland merged with British Motor Holdings, which had been formed by

merging Jaguar and the British Motor Corporation, so one giant manufacturer dominated the market.

Fast forward to 1980, and the municipal roll-call was very different. Following the creation of the PTEs in the years 1969-74 the largest municipal fleets – as well as some of the smallest – were now off the list. Between them the 49 survivors could muster just 5,866 buses – 70% of them double-deckers and 30% single-deckers. Of the double-deckers 92% were rear-engined, the rest front-engined, including 134 recently delivered Volvo Ailsas; of the growing legion of single-deckers 74% were rear-engined.

But there were some significant additions to the list of manufacturers. Of course the British Leyland

ABOVE The Leyland/Bristol share exchange in 1965 brought Bristol and Eastern Coach Works products onto the open market, and several municipals rushed to buy Bristol chassis or ECW bodies – or both, in the case of buses like this 1978 Burnley & Pendle Bristol VRTSL3 with 74-seat ECW body, seen in 1996. Gavin Booth

LEFT Alexander's bodies became increasingly popular with municipal and other fleets outside its home market in Scotland, and the company quickly became one of the country's leading bodybuilders. Lancaster bought Leyland Leopards with 53-seat Alexander Y-type bodies, among them this 1977 example seen in 1981. Gavin Booth

ABOVE Willowbrook bodies were popular with some municipal fleets. This 1973 Brighton Corporation Leyland Atlantean AN68/1R with 73-seat Willowbrook body is seen in Brighton in 1982. Gavin Booth

family, now including Bristol, dominated the list, with 91% of municipal buses at the end of 1980, but there were new names, like Foden, MCW, Scania, Seddon and Volvo; some, like Seddon and, particularly, Foden, would enjoy only brief success, but MCW became a major player in the British bus market, and Scania and Volvo are still very much with us.

The rise of Swedish imports like Scania and Volvo, along with the other makes from mainland Europe that would eventually be figuring in municipal fleets, like DAF, MAN and Mercedes-Benz, started as a revolt against Leyland's market dominance, yet while British manufacturers like Foden and Seddon also saw the opportunity, the greatest success story has been Dennis, which in the 1950s was still a low-volume builder with a select group of customers but emerged in the 1970s with a growing range of innovative chassis and is now the UK's largest bus builder, as part of Alexander Dennis.

In 1967 the seven largest municipal operators had been the major city fleets, Birmingham (1,561), Manchester (1,291), Glasgow (1,232), Liverpool (1,151), Sheffield (746), Edinburgh (698) and Leeds (673) mustering 7,352 buses between them. By 1980 only Edinburgh (by now renamed Lothian) remained in municipal hands, and this survives today as the largest of the municipal companies. The top seven in 1980 were Lothian (601), Nottingham (381), Cleveland (257), Hull (248), Leicester (232), Grampian (227) and Cardiff (218), these fleets totalling just 2,164 buses.

The PTE fleets were quick to recognise the need for a high degree of standardisation, particularly those that had inherited a very mixed bag of buses from the municipalities they absorbed. SELNEC PTE found itself with more than 2,500 buses representing dozens of different chassis and body combinations, for, even in the Greater Manchester conurbation, where the municipalities worked in broadly similar territory and often on joint services, there was no consensus about whether buses should be double- or single-deck, and even the newest double-deckers were a mix of rear-engined and front-engined types.

Geography often tended to influence municipal bus-buying patterns, and whilst it made practical sense to buy locally built products there was often a good political reason for buying from factories that employed local people. So around Manchester, Leylands, built 30 miles away, were inevitably popular, but some fleets had favoured AECs and Daimlers, both built well out of the area, although for Manchester Corporation there had been a long tradition of multi-sourcing of new buses to avoid relying completely on one supplier. Hence Manchester had bought large batches of front-engined Daimlers and Leylands with Burlingham and Metro-Cammell bodies and went on to buy many rear-engined Daimler Fleetlines and Leyland Atlanteans with Metro-Cammell and Park Royal bodies; examples of all of these passed into the SELNEC fleet. Other SELNEC constituents provided front-engined Daimler or

Leyland double-deckers, sometimes both (Ashton, Bolton, Bury, Leigh, Oldham, Ramsbottom, SHMD, Salford and Stockport), while front-engined AEC double-deckers came from Bolton, Leigh and Rochdale. Most fleets had operated Atlanteans and/or Fleetlines, though Leigh's, Ramsbottom's and Stockport's newest double-deckers were front-engined types. Although the larger fleets often went for bodywork built in the Midlands by Metro-Cammell and in the London area by Park Royal, others favoured more local products. Ashton and Oldham bought from Roe at Leeds; Ashton, Bolton, Bury, Leigh, Oldham, Ramsbottom and Stockport bought from East Lancs at Blackburn and its associate in Sheffield, Neepsend. Northern Counties, of Wigan, which would become a major supplier to SELNEC and Greater Manchester, was favoured by Ashton, Oldham and SHMD and also by Wigan, which became part of GMPTE in 1974.

Four of the fleets that made up West Midlands PTE had latterly tended to buy locally produced Daimler Fleetlines, often with locally built Metro-Cammell bodies, although Coventry used a wider range of suppliers, including Eastern Coach Works – also favoured by West Bromwich. For its unusual short Fleetlines Walsall went to Northern Counties. Wolverhampton Corporation inevitably bought locally built Guy Arab chassis.

Merseyside PTE inherited front- and rear-engined Leylands from Birkenhead, Liverpool and Wallasey, as well as Daimler Fleetlines from Birkenhead, and also took delivery of rear-engined single-deckers – Leyland Panthers and Bristol REs – that had been ordered by Liverpool. The later Merseyside PTE constituents, St Helens and Southport, brought older AEC and Leyland double-deckers, as well as some recent Atlanteans (from Southport) and a fair number of rear-engined single-deckers – AEC Swifts from St Helens and Leyland Panthers from Southport.

Tyneside PTE was dominated by Newcastle's Leyland Atlanteans but also inherited Daimlers from South Shields and, later, Sunderland, along with rear-engined single-deckers – Bristol REs from South Shields and AEC Swifts, Bristol REs and Leyland Panthers from Sunderland, which had moved away from double-deckers.

Of the second generation of PTEs, West Yorkshire inherited many Leeds-built Roe bodies from Huddersfield and Leeds corporations, typically on Daimler or Leyland chassis, as well as Alexander-bodied Atlanteans and Fleetlines from Bradford and Northern Counties-bodied Fleetlines from Halifax. Again there was evidence of a move to rear-engined single-deckers at Bradford, Halifax, Huddersfield and Leeds, with mainstream AEC, Daimler and Leyland chassis as well as Oldham-built Seddon RUs for Huddersfield.

South Yorkshire PTE inherited rear-engined Daimler and Leyland double-deckers from Sheffield (Atlanteans and Fleetlines) and from Doncaster and Rotherham (Roe-bodied Fleetlines) as well as Bristol VRTs from Sheffield. Again, rear-engined single-deckers had latterly been popular, at Doncaster

ABOVE East Lancs, based in Blackburn, had a faithful band of municipal customers, and its bodywork appropriately adorns these Blackburn Leyland Atlanteans, seen in 1981. The red roofs reflect the absorption of the Darwen municipal fleet. The prominent bus is a 74-seat 1981 **AN68C/1R.** Gavin Booth

RIGHT Northern Counties grew in importance as a bodybuilder with attractive products like this body on a 1982 Leyland Olympian 71-seater, acquired by Chester from Derby in 1987 and seen in 2002. Tony Wilson

BELOW Leeds City Transport favoured locally built Roe bodies, as on this 1974 78-seat Leyland Atlantean AN68/2R in Leeds in 1975. Gavin Booth

(Seddon RUs) Rotherham (RUs and Fleetlines) and Sheffield (AEC Swifts).

At Greater Glasgow PTE things were simpler, the undertaking inheriting Glasgow Corporation's large fleet of Alexander-bodied Atlanteans, along with many older Alexander-bodied AECs, Daimlers and Leylands.

Many municipalities recognised the importance of supporting local employment and the local economy by buying locally built bus chassis and bodywork; indeed, whilst the tendering processes sometimes steered them in different directions, it is interesting to note how often the tenders submitted by local companies won the day.

The most significant chassis manufacturers in the 1950s and 1960s were based in London (AEC), Coventry (Daimler), Wolverhampton (Guy) and Leyland (Leyland, of course). The great majority of buses were supplied by these manufacturers, but there was some loyalty to the smaller manufacturers. Sunderland bought Atkinson chassis, for instance, while Newport bought Dennis single-deckers before Dennis produced its open-market version of the Bristol Lodekka, the Loline, and this appeared in a number of municipal fleets where low-height buses were needed, like Leigh, Luton, Middlesbrough and Reading.

There was a much greater choice of bodybuilders to match the long British tradition of buying chassis from one manufacturer and bodies from another, often situated hundreds of miles apart, and hundreds of miles from the customer's home town. In the days when chassis were driven to bodybuilders a bus could well have clocked up hundreds of miles before it reached its customer. Before the advent of integral buses like the Leyland National the concept of one-stop shopping did not appear to be popular in Britain. The nearest many operators came to this was when Leyland built its own bodies for its own chassis, but when Leyland closed its bodyshop in 1954 many municipal customers had to look elsewhere.

As with chassis there was a hierarchy of bodybuilders. There were giants like Metro-Cammell and Park Royal, with substantial factories geared up for series production for major customers, as well as a thriving export business. But their factories attracted the large orders – like London Transport's postwar RT family, built mainly at Park Royal as well as by Metro-Cammell and its associated company, Weymann. This meant that orders from smaller customers could not always be squeezed in, so there was a further tier of builders, many with long-standing customers. And

ABOVE The Leyland National heralded the end of a number of Leyland's rear-engined chassis and, as an integral, represented lost orders for bodybuilders. This 1978 Chesterfield National was new to Lancashire United and is seen in 1989. Gavin Booth

there were the smaller builders whose annual output was measured in the hundreds but who attracted repeat orders from a loyal band of municipal operators. And while the major bodybuilders handled orders from the BET-group companies and London Transport, there were builders like East Lancs, Northern Counties and Roe that became closely associated with the municipal sector.

Metro-Cammell, based in the West Midlands, built for the larger municipal fleets like Birmingham, Blackpool, Coventry, Edinburgh, Liverpool, Manchester, Newcastle, Plymouth and Salford. Surrey-based Weymann built for customers like Bournemouth, Brighton, Chesterfield, Hull and Portsmouth.

London-based Park Royal built for big fleets like Birmingham and Manchester, as well as loyal customers like Barrow, Ipswich, Reading, Southampton and Swindon.

Leeds-based Roe, a sister company to Park Royal, had a firm hold on much of the Yorkshire market, as a supplier to municipal fleets like Doncaster, Huddersfield and Leeds, and further afield to Ashton, Darlington, Derby, Lincoln, Northampton, Oldham, South Shields and Sunderland, among others.

A sizeable bodybuilder that built for a very specialised group of customers was Walter Alexander.

The Scottish Bus Group companies were its principal customers, but it had built bodies for the four Scottish municipalities, though it only really had the capacity to expand this business when it moved to its new factory in Falkirk, in 1958. Thereafter it could compete with other builders – notably Metro-Cammell and Weymann – which had successfully sold into Scotland. A few English and Welsh municipals tried Alexander around this time and came back for more, as Alexander grew to become one of the two main UK-based bodybuilders.

There were clusters of bodybuilders in some areas, notably north-west England, perhaps due to the proximity of the Leyland plant. Wigan boasted two – Massey and Northern Counties – while East Lancs built its bodies in Blackburn. All three tended to concentrate on double-deck bodies, which was what the market tended to want. Massey, although its annual output was limited, not only sold to local customers like Birkenhead, Chester, Morecambe, St Annes and Wigan but also attracted orders from municipals in the South, like Exeter, Maidstone and Southend, and in Wales, like Bedwas & Machen and Caerphilly. Northern Counties, not surprisingly, also supplied bodies to Wigan Corporation, and other regular customers included Burnley Colne & Nelson,

Halifax, Middlesbrough, Nottingham, Reading, SHMD, Southend and Walsall. East Lancs was in many ways the archetypal municipal bus bodybuilder, producing solid bodies for local customers like Blackburn (of course), Bolton, Darwen, Haslingden, Lancaster, Leigh, Ramsbottom, Rawtenstall, St Helens, Todmorden, Warrington and Widnes, as well as for more distant municipals like Cardiff, Merthyr Tydfil, Portsmouth, Reading and Southampton. When Leyland closed its bodyshop, many customers turned to East Lancs.

Three significant British coachbuilders – Burlingham, Duple and Plaxton – also supplied the municipal bus market, though often they mainly built bus bodies in the summer, after the season's luxury coaches had been delivered. Burlingham was bought by Duple, and Duple ultimately by Plaxton, but not before they had supplied bodies on the growing fleet of single-deckers, in the case of Duple and Plaxton, while Burlingham had supplied both single-deck and double-deck bodies to a range of customers including Blackpool, Manchester and Reading.

Then there were significantly smaller builders, many of them a consequence of the post-World War 2 boom in bus and coach travel, which spawned a number of local firms that were able to provide much-needed capacity but which faded away as the bus market settled down. These included D. J. Davies of Merthyr Tydfil and Longwell Green of Bristol, building largely for Welsh operators.

While some municipal bus operators had a single favoured bodybuilder, the need for body contracts to go out to tender meant that several fleets were unable to standardise on one supplier – although some seemed to find ways around this. There was also the situation where customers placing substantial orders preferred to dual-source their bodies, partly because of capacity and delivery constraints but also, one suspects, to keep bodybuilders on their toes.

As several of the larger builders changed direction or became victims of 'rationalisation', new names appeared. Leyland closed down its Eastern Coach Works, Park Royal and Roe plants in the 1980s, and MCW turned first to integral buses like the Metrobus and Metrorider before concentrating on rail vehicles. Massey was bought by Northern Counties, which in turn was bought by Plaxton, which closed the Wigan plant in 2005. East Lancs found itself in the same group as Optare, a new name that had grown from the ashes of the Roe factory in Leeds. Others names came and went – Duple, Plaxton, Marshall, Pennine, Strachans, Wadham Stringer, Willowbrook – and new names appeared, most notably Wright, based in Ballymena, in Northern Ireland.

ABOVE Volvo emerged as an important supplier to the UK market in the 1970s, while Marshall, best known for its single-deck bodies, turned briefly to building double-deck bodies. This mid-engined Volvo Citybus with 78-seat Marshall body was supplied to Derby City Transport in 1984.
Gavin Booth

Chapter Four

PASTURES UNKNOWN

ABOVE Reading Transport took advantage of coach-service deregulation by introducing its X1 service linking Reading and London. A 1984 MkII MCW Metrobus 66-seater is seen in Central London in 1987. Gavin Booth

The road-service licensing system had regulated Britain's bus and coach services since the 1930 Road Traffic Act had brought some order out of the many different local rules that were applied to the fast-growing bus industry. For half a century bus and coach operators could only introduce new services or increase fares by applying to the local Traffic Commissioner, and anyone could (and did) object, which prompted a public hearing where operators had to justify their application and objectors could voice their dissent. It could be a lengthy and costly process, but one that virtually guaranteed incumbent operators – often those that were in place after the 1930 Act through 'grandfather rights' – a local monopoly, at least as far as bus services were concerned. It could be more difficult when the applications involved long-distance coach journeys, as British Rail had the right to object to new routes or increased frequencies.

Following the Conservative general election victory in 1979 it became clear that regulation and nationalisation were not likely to be in favour and that deregulation and privatisation were very much on the new Government's agenda. For a bus industry that had grown up in a regulated environment this was a shock, though there were many, often younger, managers who relished the idea of the freedom that a competitive bus market would bring. The possibility of privatisation was also perceived as both a threat and an opportunity. With six out of every ten British buses in 'public' hands – London Transport, the PTEs, National Bus Company,

Scottish Bus Group and, of course, municipalities – privatisation would have a significant impact. Who would want to buy bus companies? How would they raise the money? Again, there were managers who saw this as a great opportunity to show the world that they could run their own bus companies, perhaps build these into groups, perhaps become multi-millionaires in the process.

In fact the bus industry was not performing well, and many managers felt frustrated that they seemed only to be managing decline and were denied the opportunity to build a better network of services. Bus-passenger journeys had been in decline following the end of the post-war travel boom in the 1950s. During the 1970s alone, passenger journeys on local services had dropped by 30%, 'public' companies carrying nearly 97% of all passengers; vehicle numbers, however, had dropped by only 4.9% over the same period, and in spite of the spread of driver-only operation, staff numbers had dropped by only 12.9%.

Clearly, something had to be done to stem the decline in passengers and the constant cost increases, but nobody could have anticipated how much the industry would change.

The first move was to deregulate longer-distance express-coach services, with effect from October 1980, and although National Express emerged from this as the dominant operator, several municipals saw the opportunity to introduce coach services, such as the Reading and Southend services from these towns to London.

BELOW At the Reading terminus of the Reading-London service in 1983, a 68-seat MCW Metrobus delivered the previous year. Gavin Booth

It soon became clear that deregulation was not going to stop with express services and that the Thatcher Government was determined to see all bus services in Britain – outside London, 'for the time being' – open to competition to improve services and cut costs. And privatisation would not be too far behind, as the Government felt that publicly owned bus services were expensive, inefficient and unresponsive to the needs of the travelling public.

The appointment of Nicholas Ridley as Secretary of State for Transport in 1983 meant that deregulation of local bus services and privatisation of the publicly owned industry became inevitable. Ridley said: 'The introduction of competition into local bus services will put the emphasis on the customer rather than the operator. It will bring the opportunity for lower fares, new services, more passengers and better value for money for the ratepayer and taxpayer. The present system of regulation ... has stifled the flexible and innovative approach.'

Ridley saw the deregulated bus market as one where drivers owned their own buses, as they did in Peru and Malta, and reportedly asked a local bus manager 'How many of your drivers own their own buses?' The answer was that none of them did, but Ridley suggested that the manager should think about it. As we know, this never really happened, but it does indicate a lack of understanding about how things worked in the bus business.

What we do know is that the deregulation of local bus services in Britain – outside London – happened officially in October 1986, although the market had been in limbo for some months beforehand.

Municipal operators found themselves defending territory that had been theirs since tramway days while looking at ways they could expand their networks with this new-found freedom. The pre-deregulation situation in most of the 49 towns and cities that still had municipal bus fleets was usually fairly well defined. The corporation buses worked mainly within the urban boundary, while company buses, usually NBC fleets, worked into the towns from the outlying areas. In some cases there were restrictions on the ability of company buses to pick up and set down inside an agreed area, while in others the company buses had to charge higher fares for urban journeys to protect the incumbent municipality. At a stroke, all of this was thrown to the wind, and more than half a century of protected monopolies gave way to what in some areas was a free-for-all.

As if deregulation were not enough, the Government decided that the state-owned National Bus Company should be broken up and sold, and that the 46 remaining local-authority bus fleets should be managed by arm's-length companies.

It is appropriate at this point to list the 46 remaining fleets in local-authority control. From the north of Scotland to the south of England, the survivors were: Grampian Regional Transport Ltd (Aberdeen), Tayside Public Transport Co Ltd (Dundee), Lothian Region Transport PLC (Edinburgh), Hartlepool Transport Ltd, Cleveland Transit Ltd, Darlington

BELOW Maidstone also dabbled with express operation into Central London. This rare Bedford YNT with 49-seat Wright Contour body is pictured displaying 'City Flyer' branding at Gloucester Road, London, when still fairly new in 1984. Tony Wilson

ABOVE Rhymney Valley was renamed Inter Valley Link, using the Rhymney Valley colours in a different application. This Leyland Olympian with East Lancs body is pictured at Leyland during the 90th-anniversary celebrations for the Leyland company in 1986. Gavin Booth

Transport Co Ltd, Barrow Borough Transport Ltd, Lancaster City Transport Ltd, Burnley & Pendle Transport Co Ltd, Blackpool Transport Services Ltd, Fylde Borough Transport Ltd (Lytham St Annes), Kingston-upon-Hull City Transport Ltd, Preston Borough Transport Ltd, Blackburn Borough Transport Ltd, Hyndburn Transport Ltd, Rossendale Transport Ltd, Halton Borough Transport Ltd (Widnes), Warrington Borough Transport Ltd, Grimsby-Cleethorpes Transport Co Ltd, Lincoln City Transport Ltd, Chester City Transport Ltd, Chesterfield Transport Ltd, Nottingham City Transport Ltd, Derby City Transport Ltd, Leicester CityBus Ltd, Great Yarmouth Transport Ltd, Northampton Transport Ltd, Ipswich Buses Ltd, Merthyr Tydfil Transport Ltd, Colchester Borough Transport Ltd, Islwyn Borough Transport Ltd, Cynon Valley Transport Ltd (Aberdare), InterValley Link Ltd, Taff-Ely Transport Ltd, Newport Transport Ltd, Southend Transport Ltd, Thamesdown Transport Ltd (Swindon), Reading Transport Ltd, Cardiff City Transport Services Ltd, Maidstone Borough Transport (Holdings) Ltd, Southampton City Transport Ltd, Portsmouth City Transport Ltd, Brighton Borough Transport Ltd, Eastbourne Buses Ltd, Bournemouth Transport Ltd and Plymouth Citybus Ltd.

The shape of the British bus industry was changing dramatically as the 1980s progressed. The sale of NBC's 55 bus-operating subsidiaries was complete by 1988, and 36 of these went to their management teams, a few ostensibly with employee involvement. Of the rest, Stagecoach and Drawlane got three each, ATL

got two, and Frontsource got Alder Valley and a portfolio of engineering companies. These were new names in the bus industry, companies that recognised the potential of buying up bus companies with a view to creating successful, profitable businesses. Stagecoach, of course, went on to become an international transport giant, and while others came and went, the seeds that eventually blossomed as Arriva and First also grew out of the privatisation process.

The PTEs were next to sell off their bus-operating companies, between 1988 and 1994, and then the Scottish Bus Group companies were sold off in 1990/1; again, many of these first went to management teams, but, faced with the harsh economic realities of bus operation, all were sold on to the emerging major groups.

For some local authorities the prospect of raising substantial sums from the sale of their arm's-length bus companies was tempting, and there was no shortage of interested parties who recognised the value of an urban bus operation.

The first sales did not always go smoothly.

From 1987 Portsmouth City Transport had faced competition from Red Admiral, which was a joint venture involving Southampton Citybus and the growing Badgerline group, and in 1988 the undertaking was sold to a consortium of Portsmouth employees and Southampton Citybus, then still in municipal control. Early in 1990 the Stagecoach group bought Portsmouth Citybus, which complemented its 1989 purchase of Southdown, formerly an NBC subsidiary. Enter the Monopolies and Mergers

ABOVE A Portsmouth Corporation memory: a 1955 Leyland Titan PD2/12 with 59-seat Metro-Cammell bodywork, at Southsea.
Tony Wilson

Commission, which was taking a close interest in the rapidly changing ownership of the bus industry, but after an investigation it concluded that the takeover, although judged to be against the public interest, had not caused any adverse effects. The Government disagreed, so Stagecoach was forced to divest its Portsmouth operations, which were sold in 1991 to Transit Holdings, itself set up as a result of the privatisation of NBC's Devon General subsidiary, and a pioneer of minibus operation. Transit Holdings proceeded to recast the Portsmouth bus network using minibuses. In 1996 the business was bought by FirstGroup and merged with other local operations.

Portsmouth Corporation Tramways Department had taken over private horse trams in the town in 1901, and was operating electric trams later the same year. It bought its first bus in 1919 but replaced its trams in the mid-1930s with trolleybuses, which last operated in 1963. The Portsmouth motor-bus fleet was dominated by Leylands, but in the early postwar years Portsmouth also bought Crossleys. For years Weymann was the favoured body supplier, but latterly Alexander and East Lancs bodies were bought.

Taff-Ely Transport Ltd, based in Pontypridd, was acquired in 1988 by National Welsh, an NBC subsidiary that had been formed 10 years previously by the merger of two existing NBC fleets, Western Welsh and Red & White, and sold to its management in 1987. National Welsh went for high-frequency minibuses in a big way, but, facing heavy competition, it encountered financial difficulties and appointed receivers in 1991/2. In 1989 National Welsh had also bought InterValley Link, the arm's-length company formed to run those buses that were previously the responsibility of Rhymney Valley District Council. National Welsh was the most significant casualty of the early years of deregulation.

Taff-Ely's roots were in Pontypridd Urban District Council Transport Department, which bought into a local tramway operator in 1904, electrified the local routes and then replaced the trams from 1930, first with motor buses and then with trolleybuses; the last trolleybus ran in 1957. Pontypridd favoured Bristol chassis while these were available on the open market, moving on to Guy single-deck and double-deck models, then AEC Reliances and Regents, including the last Regents to enter service on the British mainland, in 1967. From 1973 Pontypridd (Taff-Ely from 1974) bought Leyland Nationals.

Merthyr Tydfil Transport was another casualty of the bus wars in South Wales. It was sold to a consortium of local independent bus operators, but competition from National Welsh – and retaliation against this – caused financial problems, and Merthyr Tydfil Transport ceased trading in 1989.

Like Pontypridd (and Aberdare and Cardiff), Merthyr Tydfil had favoured Bristol chassis in the 1940s, moving on to Leylands in the 1950s; latterly it ran Leyland Nationals and single-deck Dennis Dominators, and, in a final flourish, in the years 1987-9 it took delivery of 18 Leyland Lynxes.

ABOVE In the 1960s Portsmouth moved on to Metro-Cammell-bodied Leyland Atlanteans; this one, seen at Southsea in the brighter livery of the 1970s, was a 76-seater, new in 1966. Tony Wilson

LEFT In 1982 Bournemouth Transport adopted the fleetname Yellow Buses, as worn by this 1970 Alexander-bodied Leyland Atlantean PDR1A/1 in Christchurch in 1985. Tony Wilson

FACING PAGE ABOVE When London prematurely disposed of its large fleet of Daimler/Leyland Fleetlines several municipalities bought these relatively new buses to upgrade their fleets. This is a 1977 ex-London Fleetline/Metro-Cammell with Barrow Borough Transport in 1983. Tony Wilson

FACING PAGE BELOW Another customer for former London Fleetlines was Grimsby-Cleethorpes; this 1976 Leyland FE30ALR with 68-seat Park Royal body was photographed in 1989. Tony Wilson

ABOVE The most northerly municipal fleet was Aberdeen Corporation, which had become Grampian Regional Transport in 1975, an arm's-length limited company being formed in 1985. Under regional control an orange band had been added to the traditional green/cream. This late-model Leyland Atlantean AN68 with Alexander 74-seat body is seen in Aberdeen's Union Street in 1981; the cars suggest there was some kind of vintage-car run in the city at the time. Gavin Booth

Chapter Five
MORE SELL-OFFS

ABOVE A Bristol LHS6L with 30-seat ECW body, supplied to Northampton in 1979 and seen in 1982. Tony Wilson

The other sales of arm's-length municipal companies in 1989 were very different, with none of the drama that attended the early post-deregulation sales.

Grampian Regional Transport was the former Aberdeen municipal undertaking, with a fleet of 225 buses. In 1989, with privatisation of the state-owned Scottish Bus Group looming, Grampian engineered a buy-out, the first of the three Scottish local-authority fleets to be sold in this way, and the following year its parent company, GRT Holdings, made a successful bid for SBG's Midland Scottish company; then, in fairly quick succession, it acquired Eastern Scottish and Eastern Counties from their respective management teams, and, from the municipal sector, Leicester CityBus and Northampton Transport. More significantly, in the light of subsequent events, GRT merged with the Badgerline group in 1995 to create FirstBus, which would later be renamed FirstGroup in order to reflect its broader interests.

Aberdeen Corporation had operated trams from 1898, electric from 1899, then motor buses from the early 1920s. The last trams ran in 1958, and Aberdeen was one of the last British cities to convert wholly to motor buses. Its bus fleet was sourced from AEC and Daimler in the postwar years, many buses carrying Crossley or Metro-Cammell bodies, but it switched to Alexander bodies in the 1960s and latterly bought Alexander-bodied Leyland Atlanteans and Olympians.

Derby City Transport was sold in 1989 to a consortium of management and employees, the employee-owned Luton & District company taking a 25% shareholding. In 1994 British Bus, the renamed Drawlane company, bought Luton & District, and Derby shareholders agreed to sell their shares to British Bus, which had also bought the Colchester and Southend municipal companies (in 1993), whilst the Maidstone operations of Maidstone Boro'line, the fleetname adopted by the arm's-length Maidstone

company, had passed to British Bus's Maidstone & District company (in 1992). Boro'line had expanded into London tendered operations and had run into financial difficulties; Kentish Bus bought the London operations. British Bus was itself bought by Cowie Group and renamed Arriva in 1997.

Derby Corporation had bought a private horse-tramway system in 1899 and electrified it between 1904 and 1907. The trams were replaced by trolleybuses in the 1930s and continued to operate until 1967. Motor buses joined the fleet from 1924, and Daimlers were favoured; later examples of these were joined by Volvo Ailsas, Dennis Dominators and Leyland Olympians.

Barrow Borough Transport ceased trading in 1989 following a lengthy battle with Stagecoach's Ribble company, which continued to operate the Barrow routes.

Barrow-in-Furness Corporation Transport had acquired the local BET-owned tramway company in

ABOVE The new owners of former municipal companies are sometimes aware of their heritage and will mark anniversaries with modern buses wearing traditional colours. This Stagecoach Hull Dennis Trident/Alexander ALX400 is painted in the distinctive swooping blue/white livery to mark the 110th anniversary of the Corporation's transport department in 2006.
Mark Lyons

LEFT First Eastern Counties painted this former London AEC Routemaster in blue/cream Great Yarmouth-style livery to operate in the town. It is seen in Norwich in 2006.
Richard Godfrey

1920, introduced motor buses in 1923 and replaced the last trams in 1932. Barrow was a faithful Leyland fan, buying nothing else for many years. Later it turned completely to single-deckers – Leyland Leopards and Nationals, Daimler Fleetlines and Dennis Dominators – but in 1983/4 it bought some late-model Leyland Atlantean double-deckers.

The only sale of a municipal company in 1990 was of Chesterfield Transport, which was sold to its management; it would be sold on to Stagecoach in 1995.

Chesterfield Corporation had acquired a local horse-tram route in 1897, electrified it in 1904 and closed the tramway in 1927 in favour of trolleybuses, although these lasted only 11 years. Motor buses had first been bought in 1914. In the 1960s the Corporation favoured AEC single-deckers and Daimler and Leyland double-deckers; a later move to more single-deckers introduced Dennis Falcons and Leyland Nationals to the fleet.

The only other Scottish municipal company to be sold (Lothian Buses remaining resolutely council-owned) was Tayside Public Transport, the former Dundee Corporation undertaking, which was bought by its management in 1991 but acquired by National Express in 1997.

Dundee Corporation had taken over a local private tramway (operating horse, steam and electric trams) in 1899 and continued to run electric trams until 1956. Dundee briefly ran trolleybuses from 1912 to 1914 – the only commercial operation in Scotland – and motor buses from 1921. AECs and Daimlers became Dundee's

standard fare and remained so for many years, but as Tayside (the name adopted upon Scottish local-government reorganisation in 1975) the undertaking switched allegiance to the Volvo Ailsa, amassing a large fleet in the 1970s and 1980s as well as taking a batch of Bristol VRTs – the only examples for a Scottish municipal.

Also sold in 1991 was Cleveland Transit – previously Teesside Municipal Transport and before that the Middlesbrough and Stockton municipal fleets as well as the Tees-side Railless Traction Board. The operation was bought by its management and employees but would be sold on to Stagecoach in 1994.

The municipalities that made up Cleveland Transit had been closely connected from the start, Middlesbrough and Stockton jointly acquiring a local tramway company and continuing to run electric trams into the 1930s. Meanwhile, in 1919, Middlesbrough Corporation and Eston UDC had created the Tees-side Railless Traction Board to run trolleybuses, which continued until 1971, this being one of the last British systems to close. By now TRTB had combined with Stockton Corporation's transport undertaking to form Teesside Municipal Transport, which in turn changed its name to Cleveland Transit in 1974. Middlesbrough had run mainly Guy, Daimler and Dennis double-deckers, while Stockton and TRTB had concentrated on Leylands. The Cleveland fleet included Northern Counties-bodied Daimler/Leyland Fleetlines, Bristol VRTs and Dennis Dominators, as well as a growing fleet of Duple- and Plaxton-bodied Leyland Leopards.

BELOW A 1989 Tayside Volvo Citybus with 84-seat Alexander body in 1991, with evidence of the new ownership added to the fleetname on the side.
Gavin Booth

Lincoln City Transport was sold in 1991 to a consortium of management and employees with backing from Derby City Transport and would be sold on to the Yorkshire Traction group in 1993 (which had owned the former NBC Lincolnshire Road Car company since 1988). The Traction Group would in turn be acquired by Stagecoach in 2005.

Lincoln Corporation had purchased a private horse tramway in 1904 and electrified it by 1905. Motor buses were bought from 1920, finally replacing the trams in 1929.

In 1992 Cynon Valley Transport, the former Aberdare undertaking, was sold to Western Travel, one of the smaller groups to emerge from the NBC sell-off, and which would itself be sold to Stagecoach in 1993.

Aberdare Urban District Council operated electric trams from 1913, trolleybuses from 1914 and motor buses from 1922. The trolleybuses survived only until 1925, and the trams for a further 10 years.

The year 1993 turned out to be an important one for sales of municipal arm's-length companies. In addition to Colchester, Leicester, Northampton and Southend, already mentioned, the companies at Brighton, Fylde, Grimsby-Cleethorpes, Hartlepool, Hull, Lancaster, Preston and Southampton were sold.

Brighton Borough Transport was sold to its employees but would be bought by the Go-Ahead Group in 1997 and absorbed by Go-Ahead's Brighton & Hove company.

Brighton Corporation had started running electric trams in 1901, these being replaced in 1939 by motor buses and trolleybuses. The Brighton, Hove & District Omnibus Co also ran motor buses and trolleybuses in Brighton Corporation colours under a co-ordination agreement. The last Brighton trolleybuses ran in 1961.

Fylde Borough Transport had a less predictable history. Sold to its management in 1993, it was bought less than a year later by its neighbouring municipal company, Blackpool Transport Services, thus passing back into the local-authority sector.

St Annes UDC had bought a local private tramway operator in 1920, and in 1922 the undertaking became Lytham St Annes Corporation Tramways. Motor buses appeared in 1923, and the trams were replaced in 1937. The Fylde name was adopted in 1974.

In November 1993 Grimsby-Cleethorpes Transport was sold to Stagecoach, the group establishing a presence on the east coast of England that would be boosted by further municipal purchases over the next 13 months.

Grimsby Corporation had bought the local services of a private electric tramway company in 1925 and

ABOVE A pair of Grampian Leyland Atlanteans with Alexander bodywork in 1996 in First ownership, wearing different versions of their operator's pre-corporate livery. They date from 1982/3. Gavin Booth

RIGHT Parked in front of the Great Yarmouth garage in 1990 during an Omnibus Society Presidential Weekend, buses of three East Anglian municipalities – a 1988 Colchester Leyland Olympian ONCL10 with 72-seat Leyland body in CBT Coachways colours, a 1988 Ipswich Dennis Dominator/East Lancs 71-seater and a 1981 Great Yarmouth Bristol VRTSL3/ECW 74-seater. Gavin Booth

replaced these by 1937 with motor buses and trolleybuses. Neighbouring Cleethorpes acquired its share of the private tramway in 1936 but abandoned trams in 1937, replacing them with trolleybuses. Cleethorpes had run motor buses since 1930. In 1957 Grimsby-Cleethorpes Transport Joint Committee took over the bus services of both undertakings, withdrawing the trolleybuses in 1960.

Parts of the Lancaster City Transport business were also sold to Stagecoach in 1993, but by a slightly different route. The undertaking was put up for sale in 1992, and there was interest shown by other operators. Stagecoach had increased the level of its competition

with the Lancaster company, to the extent that a decision was taken to close the company, which ceased trading in 1993; Stagecoach acquired the depot and 12 buses. The Monopolies and Mergers Commission regarded this as a merger and launched an investigation, which resulted in undertakings restricting Stagecoach's ability to reduce fares or increase frequencies in the event of competition from other operators.

Lancaster had run electric trams from 1903 to 1930, and its early buses included battery and petrol-electric vehicles. Lancaster merged with Morecambe & Heysham in 1974 to create Lancaster District, the two

RIGHT The frontage of the Great Yarmouth garage incorporated transport motifs including what looked like a Leyland-bodied Titan PD2 and Stephenson's Rocket, seen here above two MCW Metroriders and an early Dennis Dart with Duple Dartline body, newly delivered in 1990. Great Yarmouth Transport would be sold to First in 1996. Gavin Booth

transport undertakings amalgamating to form Lancaster City Transport. Morecambe Corporation had bought a local horse tramway company in 1909 and this was never electrified, closing in 1926. Heysham UDC bought its part of the tramway in 1924. Morecambe started running motor buses in 1919, and in 1929 the two towns merged as Morecambe & Heysham.

Cleveland Transit, at the time owned by its management and employees, bought Kingston-upon-Hull City Transport in 1991, and this operation passed into Stagecoach hands when the latter bought Cleveland in 1994. Hartlepool Transport also passed to Stagecoach, in 1995, but in 1993 had been bought by its employees.

Cleveland Transit was born in 1974 out of Teesside Municipal Transport, itself created by the 1968 combination of the former Middlesbrough and Stockton-on-Tees corporations and the Tees-side Railless Traction Board. Middlesbrough and Stockton had bought their parts of a private electric tramway system in 1921, replacing the trams with motor buses in the 1930s. The Tees-side Railless Traction Board had been set up in 1919 to operate trolleybuses and, from 1924, motor buses.

Preston Borough Transport proved to be another interesting case. It was sold to its employees in 1993 and remained in employee ownership until 2009 when, following intense competition with Stagecoach, it was sold to Stagecoach. Later that year the Competition Commission ruled that the takeover had adversely affected competition in the area; Stagecoach was ordered to sell off the Preston Bus business, and in 2011 the Rotala group took over most of the services operated before the Stagecoach takeover.

Preston Corporation had started running its own tramways from the end of 1903, converting the system to electric cars the following year. It bought motor buses from 1922 and replaced the trams in 1935.

Southampton Citybus was sold to its employees late in 1993 and by 1997 had been bought by FirstGroup.

Southampton Corporation had bought the local horse-tramway company in 1898 and was running electric cars two years later. Although it had tried motor buses at a very early stage – in 1900 – bus operation really started in 1919, and the trams had been replaced by 1949.

By the end of 1993, of the 46 municipal companies that had survived until 1986 to become arm's-length companies, two had closed (Barrow, Merthyr Tydfil), two had gone down with National Welsh (Inter-Valley Link, Taff-Ely), 11 were part of post-privatisation groups (Portsmouth with Transit Holdings; Grampian, Leicester and Northampton with GRT; Colchester, Southend and parts of Maidstone Boro'line with British Bus; Lincoln with Traction Group; Cynon Valley, Grimsby-Cleethorpes and parts of Lancaster with Stagecoach), one (Hull) was owned by another municipal company (Cleveland), and nine (Brighton, Chesterfield, Cleveland, Derby, Fylde, Hartlepool, Portsmouth, Preston, Tayside) were owned by management or employees, or a combination thereof. Within a couple of years the ownership of some of these former municipals would change again, Derby finding itself under the control of British Bus, Fylde being owned by municipal Blackpool, Stagecoach having scooped up Chesterfield, Cleveland, Hartlepool and Hull, and the GRT group having amalgamated with Badgerline to form FirstBus.

After the rush to sell off municipal bus companies in 1993 things settled down. At the start of 1994 just 21 municipally owned companies survived, and we shall look in greater detail at these survivors. As this is written, just over half continue to trade in local-authority ownership, most of the others having followed their predecessors into big company ownership - a process not without drama in at least a couple of cases.

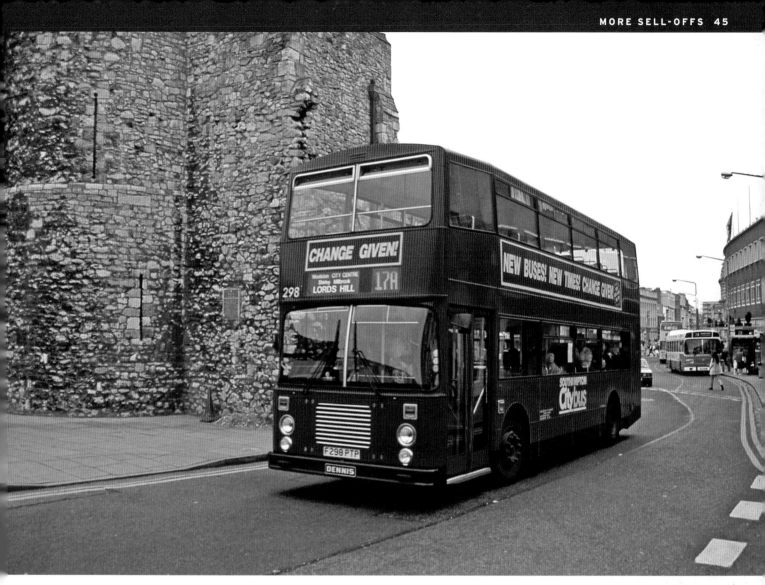

Chapter Six
THE DARLINGTON SAGA

ABOVE Roe-bodied double-deckers were Darlington's standard for many years.
This is a 1964 Daimler CCG5, photographed in 1980. Gavin Booth

Like so many municipalities, Darlington Corporation took over a privately run horse tramway and electrified it in the early years of the 20th century.

The Darlington system opened in 1904 and operated until 1924, when a fleet of 24 single-deck trolleybuses replaced 24 electric trams. So far, so typical, but Darlington was unusual, not only for its preference for single-deck trolleybuses but also because it did not operate motor buses alongside them. In fact it was 1949 before Darlington Corporation bought double-deck trolleybuses and 1950 before it bought any motor buses. Between 1950 and 1957 the five-route trolleybus system was closed, replaced by motor buses. In 1974 the undertaking was renamed Darlington Transport, and in 1986 it became Darlington Transport Co Ltd.

Darlington was also home to the head office of the once-mighty United Automobile Services company, which in 1986 had lost its Northumberland and Scarborough operations in preparation for the privatisation of its parent National Bus Company and saw its fleet total reduced from over 800 to fewer than 500 vehicles. Like many NBC companies United recognised the value of minibuses as competitive tools and introduced high-frequency hail-and-ride services in Darlington, and although Darlington Borough Council tried to sell its transport company, nothing happened, and the situation was exacerbated by the appearance of another competitor, Your Bus, which led to intensified competition from United.

Faced with heavy financial losses, Darlington Transport was put up for sale in 1994 by tender, and three companies – Yorkshire Traction, Stagecoach and Badgerline – submitted bids. Yorkshire Traction was duly named as the preferred bidder, but the situation had been complicated by the appearance of Busways on the scene. Busways Travel Services had been set up in 1986 as Tyne & Wear PTA's bus-operating company, and in 1989 it was sold to its management and employees. Looking to expand, Busways considered moving into Darlington in 1994 but during the year sold out to Stagecoach, which changed the Darlington situation dramatically.

Stagecoach registered a small network of local services in Darlington, but the Darlington Transport drivers made it known that they didn't want to work for Yorkshire Traction, preferring Busways as their new masters, so Stagecoach quickly registered all of Darlington Transport's local routes and set about recruiting the company's drivers, offering bonuses of £1,000 a head and a guarantee of three years' employment. Stagecoach was keen to start its services quickly, to keep United at bay, and started free services until the registrations came into force. This prompted Yorkshire Traction to withdraw its bid, and, unable to find another buyer, Darlington Transport went into administration in November 1994. Busways was then able to start collecting fares on its local services.

BELOW **Darlington came late to motor buses and in the 1950s and 1960s bought traditional 27ft-long rear-entrance Roe-bodied double-deckers; this is a 1964 Daimler CCG5 61-seater, still in use in 1980.** Gavin Booth

ABOVE Darlington tried various types of large single-deckers, including Daimler Fleetlines and Roadliners and rare Ward Dalesman types, as well as Dennis Dominators with dual-door 46-seat Marshall bodies, like this 1980 delivery. Gavin Booth

FACING PAGE Another Darlington Mail-bodied Dennis Dominator single-deck; this one was new in 1978 and is seen here in 1980. Gavin Booth

But that wasn't the end of the story. Your Bus stopped running in December, but local-authority concerns about over-bussing and congestion in the town led to an agreement by Stagecoach and United to reduce frequencies early in 1995.

The situation also led to an investigation by the Monopolies & Mergers Commission into the supply of bus services in north-east England, following complaints about bus services in five locations, including Darlington, which had received widespread publicity at the time of the 'bus wars'. Its report reached the following findings:

'Busways argued that DTC [Darlington Transport] had been gravely weakened by many months of predatory behaviour on the part of United Automobile Services Limited (United), by mismanagement and by the council's failure to privatise the company earlier. ... Busways submitted that its actions had prevented United from establishing a complete monopoly and had created a much healthier situation in the market, eliminating the over-bussing and congestion, which had plagued Darlington for some years.

'It is true that the people of Darlington have suffered the effects of bus wars and over-bussing for a long time, and we acknowledge that before being put up for sale DTC was indeed in a weak and declining financial state for reasons unconnected with Busways. But there was keen interest in the sale, Busways itself bidding over £1 million. It was the combination of Busways' actions in recruiting so many of DTC's drivers so quickly, registering services on all its routes and running free services which caused DTC's final collapse. We find these actions to be predatory, deplorable and against the public interest. The adverse effects which we identify are the disruption of the orderly sale of DTC and the deterrence of future competitive entry into local bus markets where Stagecoach is present, with implications not only in the reference area but elsewhere.'

In order to protect future sales of municipal bus companies the MMC proposed a moratorium on the registration of competing services during the period of sale. It decided against recommending divestment of the newly established Stagecoach operation in Darlington, which, it said, 'would be a disservice to the long-suffering townspeople'.

Darlington Transport had unwittingly become a *cause célèbre* in the annals of bus deregulation in Britain.

Chapter Seven

ACTIVITY IN THE NORTH-WEST AND EAST

ABOVE In 1979 Blackburn marked 50 years of municipal buses by painting this newly delivered 74-seat East Lancs-bodied Leyland Atlantean AN68A/1R in a lined-out traditional version of its green/cream livery. Gavin Booth

The next sales activity came in 1996, when three of the 20 remaining municipal companies passed from local-authority control. Two were in the north-west of England, which had once been home to more than 30 corporation bus fleets, but the PTEs centred on Liverpool and Manchester had assumed control of 17 of them, and at the start of 1996 there were just eight survivors – at Blackburn, Blackpool, Burnley & Pendle, Chester, Halton, Hyndburn, Rossendale and Warrington.

Stagecoach had bought Ribble, one of NBC's most charismatic companies, though at the time of purchase, in 1988, it was a smaller company than it had been a few years earlier, as a result of the Government's decision to split four geographically large companies prior to privatisation. Like United, Crosville and London Country, Ribble lost parts of its territory; some of its northern routes and depots went to its NBC neighbour, Cumberland, while a new North Western company was created, covering operations in Merseyside, West Lancashire and Wigan.

The rump of Ribble was its original heartland in Lancashire, based in Preston, and with operations running into Greater Manchester this was an important purchase for Stagecoach. At the time of the acquisition Ribble owned around 700 buses, down from almost 900 a few years earlier, but it was still a significant company by any standards. And as Stagecoach had previously bought the Cumberland company, its operations now covered a significant part of north-west England. But there were, of course, municipal operations in some of the local towns. Stagecoach managed to assume control of the Barrow and Lancaster municipal networks, and now turned its attention to Burnley & Pendle and Hyndburn.

The Burnley & Pendle municipal undertaking had its origins in 1901, when Burnley Corporation took over and electrified part of the tramway system started by a private company in 1881, using steam trams. Burnley Corporation placed motor buses in service in 1924. The

ABOVE Hyndburn was another municipality operating East Lancs-bodied Leyland Atlanteans; this 1980 AN68B/1R, looking dusty and with poorly set blinds, was photographed in 1981.
Gavin Booth

adjacent borough of Nelson had bought part of the same tramway and operated with electric cars between 1903 and 1933; Nelson Corporation bought its first motor buses in 1923. Another private tramway had been bought by Colne Corporation in 1914, motor buses being introduced the early 1920s. As Burnley, Nelson and Colne are ranged in a line, it made sense to create a new body, the Burnley, Colne & Nelson Joint Transport Committee, in 1933; the trams inherited from the three corporation undertakings had been withdrawn by 1935. In 1974, following local-government reorganisation which saw a new borough, Pendle, assume control of Colne and Nelson, BC&N was renamed Burnley & Pendle Transport.

In 1996, Pendle Council put its 50% share of Burnley & Pendle Transport up for sale, and Stagecoach beat off bids from GM Buses (North) and Preston Bus to gain control. Burnley Council was reluctant to sell its half share but threw in the towel

LEFT East Lancs bodywork again, but on 1976 Bristol VRTSL3 chassis for Burnley & Pendle, seen in 1982.
Gavin Booth

ABOVE Burnley & Pendle bought second-hand former Sunderland Corporation Bristol RELLs with 50-seat Metro-Cammell bodywork from Tyne & Wear PTE in 1977, as seen in 1981. Gavin Booth

later in 1996, allowing Stagecoach to assume full control of the undertaking.

The situation with Hyndburn Transport was more straightforward. Accrington Corporation had taken over the local steam tramway operation in 1907, replacing the steam trams with new electric cars. These ran into the towns of Haslingden and Rawtenstall, and although Rawtenstall Corporation owned its own tramcar fleet, Haslingden was happy to let Accrington and Rawtenstall run trams on its tracks. Haslingden and Rawtenstall corporations would be merged in 1968 to form Rossendale.

Hyndburn Transport was the new name (from 1974) for the Accrington municipal bus undertaking. Stagecoach took it over in 1996, absorbing it into its Ribble company and operating out of Blackburn.

Stagecoach chose to sell its East Lancashire network in 2001, and the Blackburn-based operations, along with Burnley & Pendle, were sold to Blazefield Holdings; the Blackburn operations were rebranded as Lancashire United, along with operations from Bolton and Clitheroe depots. The Burnley & Pendle operation retained this name.

In 2006 Blazefield Holdings was sold to Transdev, the French-owned group that was beginning to make acquisitions in the UK, and in 2007 Transdev bought the Blackburn Transport business, which became part of Lancashire United.

Blackburn was another Lancashire town where steam trams had operated; Blackburn Corporation had bought the private operator in 1898 and begun to electrify the system. In 1974 Blackburn absorbed neighbouring Darwen.

Today Transdev Burnley & Pendle runs 'Mainline' and 'Starship' services in and around Burnley, Colne, Nelson and Padiham, and the 'Witch Way' to Manchester. Transdev Lancashire United provides local 'Spot On' bus services in Blackburn with Darwen (as the local authority now styles itself), as well as high-quality inter-urban services linking Blackburn, Greater Manchester, Hyndburn and the Ribble Valley.

The other municipal company that was sold in 1996 was one of the two remaining East Anglian undertakings. In the post-World War 2 years there were just three municipal bus operations, at Great Yarmouth, Ipswich and Lowestoft. The main conurbations in East Anglia, which according to some definitions encompasses Cambridgeshire, include Cambridge, Norwich and Peterborough, none of which ran their own municipal buses. All, however, had tramway systems, operated by private companies. In Cambridge a plan to electrify the horse tramway was opposed by local interests, including

LEFT After Stagecoach sold its East Lancashire operations, in 2001, Blazefield resurrected the Burnley & Pendle name. The main Colne-Nelson-Burnley-Padiham route was branded 'The Mainline', running up to every 10 minutes and using 44-seat Wright Renown-bodied Volvo B10BLEs; this 2001 example is seen in Burnley in 2005.
Richard Godfrey

the university. The last horse trams ran in 1914, by which time various companies had started motor-bus services, the main survivor being Ortona, which formed an important part of the new Eastern Counties Omnibus Co in 1931. Another constituent of the new company was Peterborough Electric Traction, which had, as the name suggests, operated trams (and motor buses) in Peterborough until bought by Tilling & BAT in 1928. Norwich Electric Tramways had operated in that city until 1933, when it was acquired by Eastern Counties; the last Norwich tram ran in 1935.

As we have seen, Lowestoft's municipal bus operation, retitled Waveney District Council, had been sold to Eastern Counties in 1977, and Ipswich Buses is, in 2012, one of the 11 surviving municipal fleets.

The popular seaside resort of Great Yarmouth had introduced municipal trams in 1902, and in 1905 took over the horse tramway to neighbouring Gorleston from the British Electric Traction company. Motor buses were first bought in 1920, and buses took over the Gorleston tramway route in 1930. The last tram ran in 1933. The corporation undertaking was renamed Great Yarmouth Transport Ltd in 1986, and was acquired by FirstGroup in 1996. Although FirstGroup's roots were in municipal transport, with the Aberdeen, Leicester and Northampton undertakings under its belt, it was less interested – perhaps less successful – in buying further local-authority fleets, preferring to go after the bigger fish of the PTE companies.

LEFT The Mainline service continued after the sale of Blazefield to Transdev in 2006. In this 2011 view a 2008 Volvo B7RLE/Wright Eclipse Urban wears a new livery, complete with revised branding to reflect an enhanced frequency.
Richard Godfrey

THE BUSIER THE ROADS, THE EMPTIER THE FIELDS.

Chapter Eight
THE STORM AFTER THE CALM

ABOVE Promoting bus travel in 1979, a Bournemouth Transport Leyland Atlantean PDR1/1 with 74-seat Weymann bodywork, new in 1966. Gavin Booth

After the rush to sell – and buy – municipal bus companies in the decade following deregulation, when 28 names disappeared from the list, there was a pause for breath. Between 1997 and 2004 there was no change in the number of municipal companies, but the process restarted in 2005.

Bournemouth Corporation had started operating electric trams in 1902 after neighbouring Poole had shown that this was a successful enterprise. Bournemouth took over the lease on the Poole section, and the system expanded from Poole to Christchurch. From 1933 Bournemouth experimented with trolleybuses and decided to convert its trams with them over the next three years. There had been motor buses from 1906, used on feeder services to the trams, and the proportion grew in the 1960s as the trolleybus system was replaced, finally closing in 1969. With the undertaking generally known as Bournemouth Transport since 1974, the fleetname Yellow Buses was introduced in 1982.

In 2005 Bournemouth Transport Ltd was sold to Transdev, though not without some controversy. Wilts & Dorset, based in Poole and part of the Go-Ahead Group since 2003, was keen to expand its influence in the Bournemouth market and in 2005 had introduced services competing with Yellow Buses. At the same time Transdev had indicated its interest in buying the municipal company when Bournemouth Borough Council put it on the market, recognising the need to modernise the fleet, and this would help Yellow Buses to compete on a better footing with Wilts & Dorset, which was promising multi-million-pound investment, cheaper fares and more frequent buses, creating 'a single customer-friendly network', if it were the successful bidder. In the event, Wilts & Dorset lost out to Transdev, which bought the company at the end of 2005, leaving 10% of the shareholding with Bournemouth Borough Council. In 2011 ownership

passed to another French group, RATP.

There was no movement in 2006, and then two municipals were sold in 2007. In January, as already mentioned, Blackburn Transport was sold to Transdev, bolstering its growing presence in Lancashire. Then, in June, Chester City Council sold ChesterBus to FirstGroup, but not before there had been some high-profile competition which had resulted in ChesterBus virtually shutting up shop.

Chester Corporation had bought the local private horse tram company in 1902 and proceeded to electrify the routes from 1903. The tramway closed in 1930, replaced by motor buses. Chester City Transport had been set up in 1986.

By 2007 it had been known for a year that Chester City Council wanted to sell its bus operation, and Arriva was keen to buy it to integrate the city routes with its out-of-town services. Frustrated by lack of

LEFT Chester bought new and second-hand examples of the unsuccessful Marshall Minibus; this one, new to Chester in 1996, is seen in the city's Northgate in 2006. Richard Godfrey

ABOVE Chester latterly operated a number of Leyland Olympians, some bought new and some acquired second-hand. This Northern Counties-bodied 73-seat bus was new to Chester in 1985.
Richard Godfrey

progress with the sale, Arriva had registered the entire ChesterBus commercial network in September 2006, to start operations in January 2007, and offered to buy the undertaking. The council refused, and Arriva submitted revised registrations for two of the ChesterBus routes. A legal challenge was raised by the council, which alleged that Arriva's actions were anti-competitive. This was rejected, and Arriva launched new Chester CityBus services at the same time as First was confirmed as the successful bidder for ChesterBus, by now severely devalued by the events of the previous year.

Then Cardiff City Council announced that Cardiff Bus could be partly privatised, the council potentially selling up to 40% of the bus company. This came to nothing, but there are the precedents whereby multinational groups have taken minority shareholdings in municipal companies (Transdev at Nottingham and Keolis at Eastbourne), while Bournemouth Council

retained a 10% shareholding in Transdev Yellow Buses.

Attention then moved to the south coast, where just two municipal companies remained – Eastbourne Buses and Plymouth Citybus.

Eastbourne Buses was bought by Stagecoach in 2008 – the municipal company had been suffering from competition from Renown Coaches' Cavendish operation – which Stagecoach promptly snapped up early in 2009 in order to consolidate its position in the town.

Eastbourne Corporation had an important claim to fame: it had operated the very first continuous municipal bus service in Britain. This had started in April 1903, linking the town's railway station and the foot of Beachy Head. It never operated trams. The undertaking became Eastbourne Borough Council Transport Department in 1974 and arm's-length Eastbourne Buses Ltd in 1986.

The Eastbourne sale reduced the number of arm's-length council-owned bus companies at the start of 2009 to 13; in the 1960s the total had been more than seven times this figure.

The next sale, in 2009, was of Plymouth Citybus, and in the next chapter we shall look more closely at local resistance to the sell-off.

Plymouth had been an early municipal transport operator, buying a local horse-tram company in 1892 and electrifying its lines between 1899 and 1907. Plymouth Corporation bought out other privately owned electric-tram operators and also started bus services, in 1920; replacement of the trams started in 1930, but final abandonment was not until 1945, the city having suffered severe bomb damage in 1941.

As this is written, just 11 municipal operators remain, the most recent sale being that of the Islwyn undertaking. This tiny South Wales undertaking, based in Blackwood, had started out in 1926 as the West Monmouthshire Omnibus Board, a joint venture involving the urban district councils at Bedwellty and

RIGHT A 1992 step-entry 9.8m Dennis Dart, with rare Wadham Stringer Portsdown bodywork seating 43, in service with Eastbourne Buses in 2006.
Andy Izatt

Mynyddislwyn. In 1974 the West Mon Board became Islwyn Borough Council Transport Department, with the fleetname Islwyn Borough Transport.

In 2009 Caerphilly County Borough Council, which controlled the company following local-government reorganisation in 1996, agreed to sell the bus business to Stagecoach, and the £2.65 million deal was completed in January 2010, with 33 buses passing to Stagecoach, giving the company a 90% share of the local market. As previously noted, the former Caerphilly UDC undertaking had been absorbed in 1974 by the then new Rhymney Valley District Council, whose buses ran as Inter Valley Link Ltd from 1986 until sold to National Welsh in 1989.

ABOVE Following the Stagecoach acquisition, a fomer Eastbourne Buses MAN 14.220 with 40-seat MCV bodywork. Mark Lyons

LEFT Two MAN buses in service with Islwyn Borough Transport – an East Lancs Myllennium-bodied 14.190 bought new in 2004 and, behind, an 11.190-based Optare Vecta new to independent Tillingbourne, of Cranleigh, Surrey, in 1997 and acquired in 2001. Mark Bailey

Chapter Nine

ANATOMY OF A SELL-OFF

ABOVE Fitted with 78 seat coach seats, this East Lancs-bodied Volvo Citybus was one of a pair new to Plymouth Citybus in 1991. Mark Lyons

In May 2009 Plymouth Citybus staff were told that the City Council was looking into releasing some or all of its shares in its arm's-length company, but council leader Vivien Pengelly insisted that it would not be sold unless a 'sensible' offer were put forward. Staff were reassured that they would not be affected while discussions took place. The company, they were told, could be offered for sale by the autumn.

Almost immediately, First Devon & Cornwall and John Price, a local taxi-company owner, had expressed interest in buying the company. Marc Reddy, Managing Director of First Devon & Cornwall, said: 'We're always interested in opportunities to expand our business in the South West. If and when Plymouth Citybus is offered for sale, naturally we would be interested in it.'

Councillor Pengelly told the council: 'This process will simply see us testing the market to see what it's worth. Running a bus company is not core council business, and we're one of the few councils in the country to still own one. During these tough economic times it would be irresponsible not to find out exactly what our assets are worth, and, to do that, we need to offer it to the market. After all, something's only worth what someone's prepared to pay for it. Most councils took the decision to sell their bus companies many years ago, after deregulation in 1986. We're prepared to spark controversial debates if it means the people of Plymouth will benefit.'

And spark controversial debates they did.

First there was concern over the cost of the sale, with suggestions that it could cost up to £940,000 of public money simply to investigate the sale, and the Unite union expressed concerns about job losses and a reduction in service if the sale were to proceed, although these points were dismissed by the council as 'scaremongering'.

Plymothians were quick to rush to the defence of their bus company in the local press and on the internet. One blogger wrote:

'[The company] punches above its weight and is held in high esteem by the people of Plymouth. It pays a percentage of its profits annually as a dividend to Plymouth City Council from the profit it makes and it does make a profit. When a local bus company is taken over by a national company, the subsidies that the council pays to that company increase.

'Plymouth Citybus is community-oriented and will run buses on routes that have a small profit margin, where a national company would not. To continue running these community services after the sale of Plymouth Citybus the council would need to subsidise the routes. This negates the purpose of the sale of Plymouth Citybus.'

A 'Save Our Buses' campaign was launched, and its first leaflet posed the question 'Bloggs Bus or buses belonging to the People of Plymouth. Which would you choose?' The leaflet continued: 'Plymouth Citybus is profitable, and public transport is also one of the few areas of employment to benefit from

BELOW One of a trio of step-entry Volvo B6s, with 40-seat Plaxton Pointer bodies, bought by Plymouth in 1994. Mark Bailey

ABOVE Unusual purchases for a municipal company were 15 Mercedes-Benz O530 Citaros, delivered to Plymouth Citybus in 2005-7. Mark Lyons

an economic downturn. Selling off the firm will surely lead to a reduction in services to the community and bus routes being lost. Who would this move benefit? That's the question to ask. Ridiculously, the council claims there are "benefits for Citybus staff if a large commercial company was their employer, as working for a big company has benefits that we simply can't offer, for example, share schemes or opportunities to travel and work elsewhere." It's news to thousands of bus workers around the country! Plymouth Citybus has not only kept employment standards high, it has done this by keeping a reasonably decent public service and providing the city with a modest profit in the bargain. Basically, Plymouth citizens have a bus service at no cost to themselves. Even fare prices, though still ludicrously high, are lower than they would be with private company ownership.'

In July Citybus drivers handed councillors a petition signed by 20,000 Plymothians ahead of a meeting at which plans to sell the firm off were to be discussed. Councillor Pengelly said:

'We very much welcome the views of the public; however, I'd like to reiterate that no decision has been made at this stage. I and my party will wait to hear all the facts so that any decision we make about whether to sell Citybus will be an informed one.

'We will ensure that we take into account all views, the bids received and the potential benefits or pitfalls of a change in ownership so that we make the right decision for the whole of Plymouth.

'In the economic climate in which we are operating, this decision needs to be a rational one and not one that is responding to pressure from individuals or groups with particular perspectives.

'All councillors, regardless of the party they represent, will have the chance to cast their vote about whether to sell Citybus. The decision will be made fairly through our democratic process, once we have established all the facts.'

'People want their views put forward, and that is what we intend to do,' said Unite's regional officer, adding that 400 workers would be affected by the plans. 'Democratically elected members of the council cannot ignore the people of Plymouth and Unite's call any longer. The public petition makes it perfectly clear that the tax-paying people of this city want Citybus to stay in public hands.'

In September it was announced that Plymouth City Council had received five bids from companies interested in buying Citybus. The council insisted that inviting bids was the only way of establishing the true market value of the company. Opponents of the move claimed that the Cabinet had effectively started the privatisation process.

A council spokesperson said: 'We have received five bids by the deadline this afternoon for shares in Plymouth Citybus. We are pleased with the amount of interest we have received, and a decision on whether to continue the project is expected to be made in early October when the bids have been assessed. If the project continues, the interested companies will be invited to submit final bids.' She added that the bids would be assessed and that a report outlining the recommended way forward would go to full council in November, when a final decision on whether to sell any shares in Plymouth Citybus would be made. The council had claimed in the past that the value of Citybus was 'well in excess of £10 million'.

The local MPs got involved, and Linda Gilroy, Labour MP for Plymouth Sutton, secured a Commons debate in October. She started:

'Plymouth Citybus, with its cheerful red-and-white livery, is as much part of our great city's identity as the iconic red-and-white lighthouse that stands on Plymouth Hoe. One of the many things that makes people in Plymouth angry about the proposed sell-off of the bus company by the Conservative council is that a sale to a rival company could rob us of that distinctive part of our city's identity. People have an attachment to and an affection for their bus company. People like the red-and-white buses because Citybus has a successful track record of providing good, efficient bus services. As Jack Dromey of Unite said, it is one of the finest bus companies in the land. This debate is not about a bus company that has failed and so has to be put into the private sector.

'The company works well on prices. For example the Dayrider ticket is good value compared with those in other cities. That is possible because Citybus, as a publicly owned company, has used its competitive position to benefit everyone. It currently has 60% of the competitive market. If Citybus is sold to a rival bus company an even fiercer price war is likely, as has been seen in other cities. Although that might drive down prices and appear to be good for customers in the short term, in the longer term it would probably lead to the emergence of one dominant company. If such a company was not in public hands, as sure as night follows day, it would end up stifling competition and keeping prices high.

'It is ironic that Citybus, which is a successful recipe that delivers good outcomes to all, is being put at risk just as the problem of bus wars leading to dominant companies has emerged all over the country. There has been a market survey by the Office of Fair Trading and a consultation is ongoing on the matter. If that leads to a full-blown investigation by the Competition Commission, it would be well advised to look at how the sustainable bus services work in Plymouth.

'Citybus is a green asset that not only provides good access to public transport for a high proportion of the population but invests its profits

BELOW A 1989 Plymouth Citybus 84-seat Alexander-bodied Volvo Citybus – one of eight bought from Trent in 2000 – photographed in 2003.
Andy Izatt

to that end. It is not under pressure, as a private company would be, to distribute a higher proportion of its profits to shareholders. That means that all vehicles operate on ultra-low-sulphur diesel fuel and all new vehicles comply with the latest emission levels. It is ahead of the curve in investing in Euro 4.5 and 5 vehicles.

'Unlike most other bus companies, Citybus still employs a pool of local engineers, which is a sustainable way of ensuring high-quality maintenance and reliability. A pool of local, skilled employees ensures that engines and parts are maintained to high standards and that an environmentally unsustainable waste of parts and engines is avoided. There is also high-quality performance in terms of emissions. Most companies that might express an interest in taking over from Citybus do not have engineering or coaching as part of their core business, so both activities would be likely to stop if it were sold. That would result in the loss of 10% of the jobs. The engineering work would have to be done elsewhere, and it is unlikely that the win-win balance of engineering and sustainable maintenance practices would be preserved.

'Of course, Plymouth City Council has to raise money in the face of difficult economic circumstances and the likelihood of tighter public spending. However, I say to the Minister that it is a question of priorities, and there are other ways of saving money. The capital programme could be engineered differently, or other assets could be

sold. It says a lot about Conservative priorities in Plymouth that they have chosen to target Citybus without setting out why it is a priority for disposal over other assets.'

Gary Streeter, Conservative MP for South West Devon, said: 'I certainly accept that Citybus is a very impressive company, but does [Linda Gilroy] agree that although it is owned by the council, it is not run by the council; it is run by its own board. Why on earth would a private company spend millions on buying Citybus and then slash its routes and reduce its services in the way she has described? I am bound to ask whether she is just scaremongering and using the issue to launch her election campaign.'

Linda Gilroy responded: 'To put it simply, Citybus works. It works by providing value for money, excellent access and environmental efficiency in an age that calls for responsibility, public service and sustainability.'

In November Go-Ahead Group was named as the preferred bidder for Citybus. Completion, subject to final due diligence and full council approval, was expected at the end of the month. Keith Ludeman, then Chief Executive of Go-Ahead, said: 'We are very pleased to have been selected as the preferred bidder and are now working closely with Plymouth City Council to complete the deal. Plymouth Citybus has an excellent reputation and fits well with our strategy of investing in high-quality bus companies in urban areas which then maintain a strong local brand and high degree of autonomy to ensure close links to local customers and other stakeholders.'

BELOW A Mercedes-Benz 709D/Plaxton Beaver 25-seat minibus bought in 1995.
Mark Bailey

ABOVE In 2008 Plymouth bought 11 Alexander Dennis Enviro200s. One is seen in Royal Parade in 2009.
Richard Godfrey

Councillor Pengelly said: 'I know many people are fundamentally opposed to a change in ownership, but we owe it to people living in the city to look at the facts. We have to weigh up the pros and cons and make a decision based on what is right for Plymouth people and what makes good business sense.'

Go-Ahead already had a significant presence on the south coast, with around 850 vehicles in and around Brighton, Southampton, Bournemouth and on the Isle of Wight, as well as inland with its Wilts & Dorset business.

But that wasn't the end of it.

A march was planned for Saturday 28 November, two days before the proposed sale of Citybus was due to go before the City Council. More than 60 members of Plymouth Labour and Unite joined members of the public to demonstrate against the plans. In an introduction to a video report Linda Gilroy said: 'We have 48 hours to save Citybus. I hope that some Conservative councillors will vote with Labour on Monday and save Citybus from being sold.' Alison Seabeck, MP for Plymouth Devonport, said: 'Selling Citybus is going to cost local taxpayers money, it is going to cost jobs and it is entirely wrong that local Conservatives are doing this. If they are doing this locally, just imagine what they would do nationally.'

Councillor Tudor Evans, leader of Plymouth City Council's Labour group, said: 'From day one this process can be summed up by three words – secrets and lies. The Conservatives are trying to push through the sale of Citybus quickly and are selling the company too cheap. It is the worst deal in Plymouth's history.'

On the day of the council decision union members staged a protest outside the Council House. Mark Baskerville, the Citybus branch representative for Unite, told a group of about 30 placard-waving demonstrators: 'The company is ours. It belongs to the people of Plymouth.' He added: 'Once the ink is dry, unless there's some sort of legal process that we can follow there won't be anything we can do about the sale.'

Councillors and MPs queued up at the eleventh hour to express their concerns over the sale, but the deal went ahead, Go-Ahead paying £20.2 million; the sum received by the council, after adjustments for debt and other payments, was £19.58 million. The Citybus name remained, although Go-Ahead reserved its right to change the livery. Go-Ahead agreed to maintain the school routes operated by Citybus for at least three years and stated that other existing routes would be protected for at least six months with no changes. After that the council will be given 90 days' notice of proposed changes. There would be no compulsory redundancies for Citybus drivers on local bus services for the next 12 months.

The Office of Fair Trading subsequently decided not to investigate the purchase of Plymouth Citybus by Go-Ahead Group.

FACING PAGE ABOVE In 2009 Plymouth Citybus bought a number of ex-London General Volvo B7TLs with East Lancs Vyking bodywork, dating from 2002. Mark Bailey

FACING PAGE BELOW Following the Go-Ahead takeover Plymouth's livery was redesigned, the result being seen on this 2003 Dennis Dart/Plaxton Pointer SPD. Mark Bailey

ABOVE This 1998 Dennis Dart with Wright Crusader body was one of a number acquired by Plymouth Citybus in 2010 from fellow Go-Ahead Group subsidiary Oxford Bus Company. Mark Bailey

Chapter Ten
THE SURVIVORS

ABOVE In 2012 Lothian Buses, the UK's largest municipal bus operator, started up a new company, East Lothian Buses, to operate a route abandoned by First Scotland East. The buses initially used were Plaxton President-bodied Dennis Tridents in overall white. Gavin Booth

At the time of writing there are just 11 arm's-length municipal bus companies in Britain, though this situation could of course change; any of the councils holding shares in these companies could decide that selling the bus company could help the municipal coffers and thus stave off rises in Council Tax. As we have seen, many councils decided to do just that, often facing accusations that they were 'selling the family silver' to shore up their finances, and while some bus passengers have lost out following the sell-offs, as the new owners decided to rationalise their services, others have seen little difference, other than a change of fleetname and, sometimes, a change of livery.

A great deal depends on the corporate approach of the new owners. Where the big groups have been successful in buying municipal operators they have imposed their corporate colours, so First and Stagecoach liveries are to be found adorning the buses serving a significant number of Britain's towns and cities. Arriva, also strongly corporate, has been less active – or perhaps less successful – in the municipal market, but Arriva-liveried buses can nevertheless be found on local services in Derby and Southend.

French-owned Transdev has been actively growing its British presence, acquiring the Bournemouth and Blackburn undertakings in 2005 and 2007. Bournemouth's municipal buses had traded latterly as Yellow Buses, and Transdev retained this name and updated the yellow livery. In 2011 ownership of Yellow Buses was transferred to RATP Dev when the merger between Veolia Transport and Transdev prompted RATP to withdraw from its shareholding in the capital of Transdev.

Transdev continues to run the former Blazefield operations in Lancashire, including the operations of the two municipal companies – Burnley & Pendle and Hyndburn – that had been bought by Stagecoach in 1996 and sold on to Blazefield five years later. Blazefield sold to Transdev in 2006, and the following year Transdev bought Blackburn Transport. Here, however, old municipal liveries had disappeared, and bold new identities were developed – 'Spot On' for the local services of the Lancashire United company in Blackburn, Darwen and Hyndburn, and 'Starship' in Burnley & Pendle.

Most of the municipal operations in the populous Liverpool and Manchester areas had disappeared with the creation of the first PTEs in 1969, but a few survived and count among the 11 survivors; Halton, Rossendale and Warrington just escaped inclusion in the PTE areas. Rossendale sits just to the north of Greater Manchester's Rochdale and Bury districts, while Halton and Warrington are to the south – Halton adjoining Merseyside, and Warrington adjacent to the Merseyside and Greater Manchester boundaries. Halton and Warrington share a boundary.

BELOW Nottingham is the largest of the remaining English municipal companies, and has adopted colour-coding to distinguish groups of routes on main corridors. The Maroon Line services run to Beeston via the university, as seen on this 2004 Scania L94UB OmniTown with East Lancs 33-seat bodywork incorporating a standard Scania front-end structure. Richard Godfrey

ABOVE Dennis Super Darts dominate the Halton fleet, some with East Lancs bodies and others Marshall, the latter including this 36-seat example, new in 2001 and seen in Widnes. Mark Lyons

Halton

The borough of Halton was created in the 1974 local-government reorganisation, uniting the towns of Widnes and Runcorn, north and south of the River Mersey. Halton is the most densely populated district in Cheshire, with a population nudging 120,000.

Widnes, a long-established industrial town, houses roundly half of Halton's population, while Runcorn, also a long-established community, doubled in population terms following the creation of Runcorn New Town in the 1960s and 1970s and now broadly matches that of Widnes.

Widnes Corporation was one of the few that never owned or operated a tramway, but was an early convert to the new motor buses. It started services in 1909 using four covered-top Commers – possibly the first double-deckers in the world with covered tops, although as these were 2ft higher than the 14ft 6in that is regarded as 'normal height' today, there may have been concerns over their stability. It is suggested that the covered tops were specified due to the corrosive atmosphere and acid rain associated with the chemical factories in Widnes. The buses were used to serve the town and connect with south Lancashire's

extensive tramway network at Rainhill. Widnes Corporation Motor Omnibus Department was one of the smaller municipal bus operations in Lancashire, and like many neighbouring undertakings it favoured locally built products – Leyland chassis and East Lancs bodies. However, when Widnes joined with Runcorn in 1974, associated boundary changes placed the new borough of Halton in Cheshire.

In the late 1960s Widnes Corporation had moved away from double-deck purchases, buying Bristol RESLs and RELLs and Leyland Leopards, and in 1972 it received a very early Leyland National, the first single-door example; from 1976 Halton Transport standardised on Nationals, literally to the end of production, as it received the last National built, delivered in November 1985. The move to single-deckers was prompted partly by the need to operate on the pioneering Runcorn Busway, which can accommodate only single-deck vehicles. Halton was a loyal customer for the National's successor, the Leyland Lynx, taking its first in September 1986 and the last Lynx off the assembly line, in August 1992.

Following bus-service deregulation in 1986 Halton Transport faced competition in and around its operating area from North Western (the previous Crosville operation) and Merseybus, but it retaliated

ABOVE Halton No 1, pictured in Huyton, is a 2007 Alexander Dennis Enviro200 with 10.9m MCV Evolution bodywork.
Paul Godding

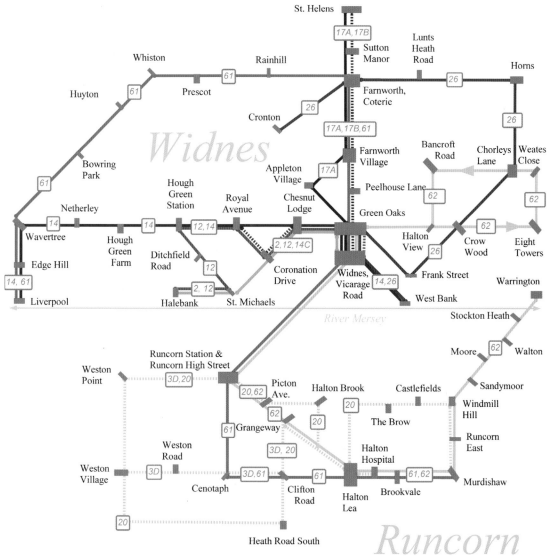

successfully with new routes and increased frequencies.

In 1987 Halton confirmed its fondness for the Leyland National by buying more than 20 from various National Bus Company fleets, including its neighbour, Crosville. It then moved on to the Dennis Dart from 1994, first taking step-entrance chassis with Marshall bodies, then 45 SLF models, also with Marshall bodies, between 1997 and 2002. From 2002 Halton moved on to Darts with East Lancs bodies; most of the Halton Darts are the longer Super Dart type. These were followed by the Dart's successor, the Alexander Dennis Enviro200, with Alexander Dennis or MCV bodywork.

Halton Transport and Arriva (the former Crosville operations) run the bulk of the bus services in Halton today, the municipal company providing links in and between Widnes and Runcorn and also into the neighbouring areas of Liverpool, St Helens and Warrington.

ABOVE Halton's more recent deliveries have been Alexander Dennis Enviro200s, including some with MCV bodies and, as here, four complete 11.3m-long Alexander Dennis 35-seaters, new in 2010. Mark Bailey

Halton's Nationals and Lynxes

For years Halton Transport's predecessor, Widnes Corporation, had been a fairly traditional north-western operator, running a fleet of East Lancs-bodied Leyland Titan PD2s, but in the late 1960s it turned to single-deckers, first East Lancs-bodied Leyland Leopards and then East Lancs-bodied Bristol RESLs.

But in 1972 Widnes bought a very early Leyland National, one of the first 100 built, and delivered in the late summer of 1972. It was the first single-door National, and it must have impressed, because Widnes/Halton went on to buy 19 more, including nine Mk2 examples; the last of these, delivered late in 1985, was the last Leyland National built.

Halton then turned to the National's successor, the Leyland Lynx, buying its first in 1986 – the first Lynx to enter service anywhere – and this was followed by 16 Lynxes between 1987 and 1989, and 18 Lynx IIs between 1990 and 1992, these including the last Lynx built.

ABOVE New in August 1992, Halton 37 was the very last Leyland Lynx to be built, a 51-seat Lynx II. Paul Godding

BELOW Three of Halton's other 1992 Lynx II deliveries photographed together. Mark Bailey

Newport

As recently as the mid-20th century there was ambiguity in the minds of many people about Monmouthshire – was it part of England or part of Wales? Now firmly established in Wales, the city of Newport is the largest settlement in Monmouthshire, with a broadly based economy benefiting from its position close to the Severn crossings and the M4 motorway.

Newport Corporation bought a local private horse tramway in 1875 and electrified it in 1903. It started running motor buses in 1924 and replaced its trams between 1929 and 1937. Daimler, Guy and Leyland chassis were favoured for many years, often with locally built bodies – by Bruce, D. J. Davies and Longwell Green. Newport also bought small batches of Dennis chassis in the 1950s. These buses were replaced by Leyland Atlanteans, Bristol RESLs and Metro-Scania single-deckers and double-deck Metropolitans. Newport also

bought MCW Metrobuses before moving to Scanias in a big way in the 1980s and 1990s. It bought Scania 112-series single-deckers with Wadham Stringer bodies and 113-series single-deckers with Alexander Strider bodies, as well as 112-series double-deckers with Alexander, East Lancs and Marshall bodies and 113-series double-deckers with Alexander bodies. Its smaller buses in the 1980s and 1990s were MCW and Optare Metroriders.

The present fleet of Newport Transport Ltd is around the 100 mark and is still dominated by Scanias – OmniCity single-deckers and Wright-bodied L94UBs, although there are also Dennis Darts, Alexander Dennis Enviro200s and Wright-bodied MANs. Double-deckers are Volvo Olympians, acquired second-hand from Lothian, and Dennis Tridents.

Newport Transport has recently revamped its image, restyling itself Newport Bus, and has expanded its route network beyond the purely town-based services, adding an express service to Monmouth to its existing services to Cardiff; it has also started local services in Monmouth.

ABOVE Newport Bus has seven Volvo Olympians with Alexander Royale bodies, acquired in 2009 from Lothian Buses. Mark Bailey

Newport's Scanias

Scania made serious efforts to break into the British bus market, first in partnership with the bodybuilder MCW and then on its own account. The Metro-Scania single-deck bus was seen as a rival to Leyland's new National and introduced many British operators to the concept of sophisticated European citybuses. This was followed by the Metropolitan double-decker, again a Scania/MCW joint venture, and then by an increasingly wide range of single-deck and double-deck underframes as Scania and MCW went their separate ways.

Newport was an early customer for the Metro-Scania and Metropolitan and went on to buy Scania chassis with a range of bodies throughout the 1980s and 1990s. Recent deliveries have included Scania OmniCity and L94 models, as well as Alexander Dennis and MAN types.

Continuing Newport's long association with Scanias, a 1998 L94UB with Wright Axcess Floline body. Mark Bailey

ABOVE Recalling earlier days at Newport, a 40-seat Metro-Scania – one of 44 bought new in 1971/2 – operating on the free Centrebus service. The Metro-Scania was a joint venture involving Scania and Metro-Cammell. Dale Tringham

FACING PAGE ABOVE One of 11 8.9m Alexander Dennis Enviro200s added to the Newport fleet in 2011/2. Mark Bailey

FACING PAGE BELOW Liveried for the X30 Newport–Cardiff service, a 2011 Scania OmniCity, one of 38 bought between 2002 and 2011. Mark Bailey

Ipswich

In terms of fleet size, Ipswich Buses is the second-smallest surviving municipal bus company, with fewer than 80 buses. It is the sole remaining municipal in East Anglia and the only one close to the east coast of England.

Ipswich is the county town of Suffolk, with a population of around 130,000, and has undergone a successful regeneration in recent years.

A private company introduced horse trams in Ipswich in 1880 and Ipswich Corporation bought the business in 1901, prompting a move to electric trams from 1903, and to trolleybuses 20 years later. By 1926 the trolleybuses had replaced the trams. Unusually, there were no motor buses in the fleet until 1950. However, as the trams had been replaced by trolleybuses, so the trolleybuses themselves gave way to motor buses between 1953 and 1963.

The trolleybus fleet had included locally built Ransomes, Sims & Jefferies types, but the motor-bus fleet was standardised for many years on Park Royal-bodied AECs, although later AECs had East Lancs, Massey and Willowbrook bodies. Ipswich bought its first Leyland Atlanteans, with locally built Eastern Coach Works bodies, in 1968 and went on to buy more Atlanteans, with Roe and East Lancs bodies, before moving on to some rarer single-deck types – the Dennis Falcon HC, with East Lancs and Northern Counties bodywork (including some second-hand

from Chesterfield), and the Bristol B21 – essentially a Leyland National chassis that was supplied mainly to Australian customers but also to Ulsterbus; Ipswich bought four new B21s and Ulsterbus six, all with Alexander (Belfast) bodies, and the Ulsterbus examples duly found their way to Ipswich.

In 1974 the undertaking had been renamed Ipswich Borough Transport, and in 1986 the arm's-length Ipswich Buses Ltd took over.

Following deregulation Ipswich bought Dodge S56 minibuses and then moved on to the Dennis Lance, with East Lancs or Optare bodywork, and the DAF SB220/Optare Delta. Like so many other municipal fleets it turned to the Metrorider, initially from MCW and then from Optare, for its small-bus requirements. It has also bought Dennis Darts and Optare Excels and Solos. More recently Ipswich Buses has bought new East Lancs-bodied Volvo Olympians and DAF DB250s with East Lancs and Optare bodies, as well as Scania N94UD/East Lancs OmniDekkas and Scania N230UDs with Optare bodywork.

The present-day network is an interesting one, comprising around 20 routes, including several that are circular, with different route numbers for inner and outer circles, and others that are linear but with extensive one-way circles at the outer end, and which are operated as complete journeys from the town centre. Daytime frequencies range from hourly services to five journeys per hour on some of the busier routes.

Ipswich's Leyland B21s

Although the integral Leyland National single-deck bus was designed to be a highly standardised product, Leyland recognised that there were markets where it was politically important to allow operators to specify locally built or at least locally assembled bodywork. So in addition to the complete National, which was bought by many British municipals, in 1975 Leyland introduced the B21 chassis, which was mechanically almost identical to the National but had a front-mounted radiator to help cooling in hot countries. Leyland saw the B21 as successor to the popular Bristol RE, and the B21 was built at the Bristol plant.

Ipswich ordered four B21s, and these were delivered in 1985 with dual-door Alexander (Belfast) bodies; the chassis were diverted from a cancelled Tel Aviv order.

The only other UK customer for the B21 was Ulsterbus, which had been treated by Leyland as an 'export' customer to allow it to continue receiving Bristol RE chassis long after other UK operators had been denied the chance to buy these. Leyland had built a fleet of six B21 for Ulsterbus and its sister Citybus to appraise in service, and these were delivered in 1981/2, with Alexander (Belfast) bodies. These buses did not last long in Northern Ireland and in 1991 were withdrawn and sold to Ipswich.

ABOVE One of the four Leyland B21s delivered to Ipswich in 1985, with Alexander (Belfast) bodywork. It carries Bristol badging, acknowledging where the chassis was built, and is named Godspeed in the municipality's tradition of naming its buses. Dale Tringham

BELOW The four B21s bought from Ulsterbus/Citybus in 1991 carried a different style of Alexander (Belfast) bodywork. This one had operated with Citybus in Belfast. Andy Izatt

Rossendale

Like Halton and Warrington, Rossendale survives as a municipal bus company on the fringes of PTE-land, where many neighbouring municipalities were swallowed up more than 40 years ago.

The borough of Rossendale was formed in 1974, combining the mill towns of Bacup, Haslingden and Rawtenstall on the west side of the South Pennines, but the Rossendale Joint Transport Committee had been formed in 1968 to run the services previously under the control of Rawtenstall and Haslingden corporations.

Haslingden was one of the smaller municipal bus operations, served in the 19th century by company-owned steam trams, but after the company was bought by the corporations of Accrington, Haslingden and Rawtenstall in 1907 Haslingden chose to stop operating trams, though these continued to run into the town after Accrington electrified its part of the system. Instead, Haslingden turned to motor buses, trying an early Leyland between 1907 and 1909 before commencing bus operation in 1920.

Rawtenstall too experimented with motor buses in the early days but in 1908 acquired parts of the privately owned steam tramway and proceeded to electrify it. Serious bus operation started in 1924, and the buses replaced the trams between 1929 and 1932.

There were close links with other small local municipals; indeed, in the post-war era Rawtenstall's General Manager was also responsible for the Haslingden and Ramsbottom undertakings. However, whereas Rawtenstall (45 buses) and Haslingden (15) eventually amalgamated in 1968 to form the Rossendale Joint Transport Committee, Ramsbottom (12) remained separate, its fleet ultimately being absorbed by the newly created SELNEC PTE in 1969.

In common with neighbouring operators, both Haslingden and Rawtenstall had standardised on Leylands for their bus fleets. Rossendale thus inherited an all-Leyland fleet, but it went on to buy Bristol LHSs and RESLs – with Leyland engines – as well as MCW and Optare Metroriders, Leyland Leopards, Tigers and Atlanteans and the inevitable Dennis Darts, many of these being second-hand acquisitions. Indeed, in the five years following deregulation in 1986 Rossendale seemed to go on a second-hand buying spree, acquiring more than 50 such buses from a variety of sources; they included Dodge, Sherpa and Metrorider minibuses, Leyland Leopards and Tigers, and Daimler Fleetlines and Leyland Atlanteans. In 1992/3 it had many of the Leopards fitted with new East Lancs EL2000 bodies. As the 1990s progressed Rossendale bought more second-hand Atlanteans, as well as Olympians and Darts.

In recent years Rossendale has continued to upgrade its fleet with a mix of new and second-hand

ABOVE Among Rossendale's earliest second-hand acquisitions, from Strathclyde PTE in 1984, were three Alexander-bodied Leyland Atlanteans dating from 1975.
Gavin Booth

Rossendale's second-hand buses

The majority of municipal operators seldom, if ever, bought a second-hand bus, but the pressures of the competition that followed deregulation forced many engineers to go out with their shopping lists to see what bargains they could pick up. And bargains there were, as some operators shed fairly recent buses and sometimes found them back in their old haunts, running in competition.

Rossendale Transport raised its game at the time of deregulation, well over 150 second-hand buses joining the fleet in the 1980s and 1990s. They ranged from ex-West Midlands PTE minibuses, through Leyland Leopards and Tigers from a range of sources, plus Daimler Fleetlines and Leyland Atlanteans from operators of all sizes, to newer Leyland Olympians and Dennis Darts. And it was these second-hand vehicles that helped Rossendale to expand beyond its traditional territory in Bacup, Haslingden and Rawtenstall.

New in 2000 to JP Travel of Middleton, Manchester, this Volvo B7TL with 76-seat East Lancs Vyking body came to Rossendale via Moffat & Williamson in Scotland. Mark Lyons

FACING PAGE ABOVE The Rossendale fleet includes four Dennis Darts with 41-seat Alexander ALX200 bodies, new in 2000 to Munro, Jedburgh, and acquired in 2006. Mark Bailey

FACING PAGE BELOW Purchased in 2005 were three MAN 14.220s with MCV Stirling bodies, new the previous year to 2Travel, Pentrechwyth. This one displays the previous style of 'Easyride' branding used by Rossendale Transport. Mark Bailey

buses. It has bought batches of Optare Solos and Volvo B7RLEs, as well as East Lancs- and Plaxton-bodied Dennis Darts, and has topped these up with further Darts acquired from local operators Blue Bus and South Lancs Travel, as well as MCV-bodied MANs from 2Travel and Scania/Wright Solars from Reading Buses. Second-hand double-deck purchases have comprised Volvo B7TLs with East Lancs bodies for the main fleet, and Northern Counties-bodied Volvo Olympians for schools work. The main fleet has been fully low-floor since 2005.

The fleet grew in the years following deregulation, partly in response to competition, and now stands at around 100 buses, including a number based in Rochdale. Its routes stretch out to other towns that once had their own municipal buses, notably Accrington, Blackburn, Bolton, Burnley, Bury, Rochdale and Todmorden. In recent years it has rebranded itself as Rossendalebus, adopting a revised livery which retains the red and cream colours that have been associated with the undertaking for so long.

In 2009 Rossendale Council investigated the possibility of selling its bus company, but after 'test marketing' it concluded that the likely sale price would not meet its expectations. In a statement released at the time it announced: 'The council will therefore retain its ownership of Rossendale Transport Limited and work with the company in the continual improvement of local services, customer standards, operational efficiencies and local employment within Rossendale. The council is grateful to the staff and customers of Rossendale Transport Limited for their comments, feedback and patience during the period of this exercise.'

LEFT Wearing the newer Rossendalebus livery is this 2007 Volvo B7RLE with 44-seat Wright Eclipse Urban bodywork. Mark Bailey

Thamesdown

Swindon grew up around the Great Western Railway junction and works that were established there in the 19th century. The Corporation started running electric trams in 1904 and motor buses from 1927, replacing the trams in 1929. Thamesdown Transport was formed as a result of local-government reorganisation in 1974, becoming in an arm's-length limited company in 1986.

The post-war fleet was dominated by Daimlers – CVG6 and, later, Fleetline models; at one time Park Royal was the favoured bodybuilder, but the Fleetlines had Northern Counties, Metro-Cammell, and, later, ECW bodies.

In the early 1980s Thamesdown turned to Dennis for double-deckers – Dominators with Northern Counties and East Lancs bodies – and bought a number of second-hand Dennis single-deckers, these being Duple- and Wadham Stringer-bodied Lancets

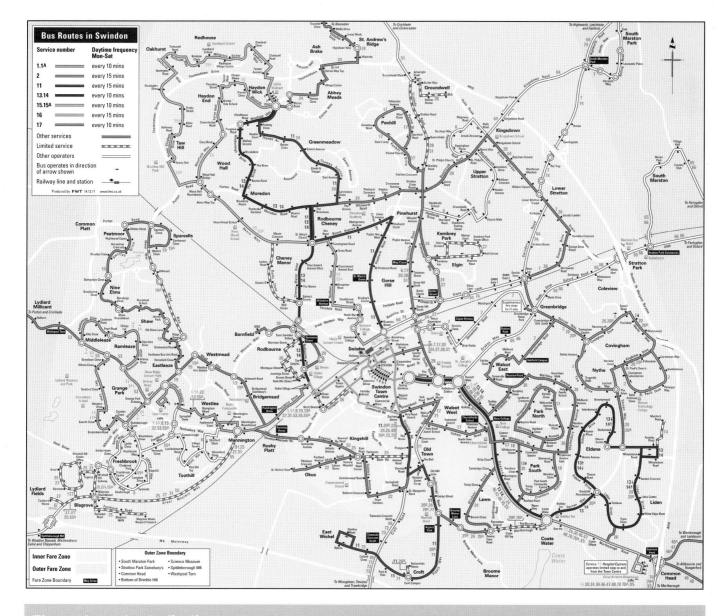

Bus Routes in Swindon

Service number	Daytime frequency Mon-Sat
1.1A	every 10 mins
2	every 15 mins
11	every 15 mins
13.14	every 10 mins
15.15A	every 10 mins
16	every 15 mins
17	every 10 mins
Other services	
Limited service	
Other operators	
Bus operates in direction of arrow shown	
Railway line and station	www.fwt.co.uk

Produced by FWT 14.12.11

Inner Fare Zone
Outer Fare Zone
Fare Zone Boundary

Outer Zone Boundary
• South Marston Park   • Science Museum
• Stratton Park Sainsbury's • Spittleborough M4
• Common Head   • Washpool Turn
• Bottom of Brimble Hill

Thamesdown standardisation

Standardisation of vehicle types has long been a goal for many operators, but, with requirements for buses of all sizes, few manage to achieve any great measure of standardisation. Sometimes this is deliberate - resulting from the need to dual-source, to avoid reliance on one supplier - or a consequence of tendering for new bus orders.

Thamesdown Transport managed to achieve a high degree of standardisation in the early years of the 21st century with a substantial fleet of Plaxton Pointer-bodied Dennis Darts, some variety being provided by Fleetline double-deckers for schools work. This is most noticeable following the opening of Thamesdown's impressive Barnfield Road depot in 2005; here buses are parked in rows according to type - an impressive sight late at night and on Sundays, when few of them are on the road.

Between 1998 and 2004 Thamesdown standardised on Dennis/Plaxton SPD Darts like this 2004 41-seater. Named Swindon, it was one of four to wear this special centenary livery. Andy Izatt

ABOVE In 2010 Thamesdown bought eight Optare Versa 37-seaters, and, like most of the company's buses, these carry names, many recalling locomotives built in Swindon by the Great Western Railway; this is King George V.
Mark Lyons

RIGHT A 2008 Thamesdown Scania K230UB/Wright Solar 40-seater, named Rougemont.
Russell Young

and Duple-bodied Falcons. It also bought additional Leyland Fleetlines, from London Transport, Greater Manchester and, later, for schools work, from Yellow Buses, Bournemouth.

Today's Thamesdown fleet is highly standardised, comprising Dennis/Plaxton Pointer SPD Darts and Scania/Wright Solars; it also includes some Optare Versas, and there is a small double-deck fleet consisting mainly of ex-Lothian Volvo Olympians, used principally for schools work.

The route network covers Swindon with higher-frequency services, but there are also less-frequent country services to Cricklade, Hungerford, Lambourn and Marlborough.

Warrington

Electric trams ran in Warrington between 1902 and 1935, and Warrington Corporation had first bought motor buses in 1913, but it only really expanded its bus fleet in the 1920s.

At the time of local-bus deregulation in 1986 the Warrington fleet consisted of just 63 buses, but since then, in the company's words, 'a policy of discreet expansion has been followed, the basic premise being that if money could be made by operating services deemed uneconomic by other operators, then WBT should assume operation. Thus, in the decade following deregulation, WBT expanded towards Leigh and Northwich on both commercial and supported services.' Warrington faced predatory competition in the 1990s, from North Western and Merseyside Transport, but it fought back, and the competing companies retrenched. The arm's-length Warrington Borough Transport company had been set up in 1986, and the operation was rebranded as Network Warrington in 2006, the year the town's new bus interchange opened.

In the post-war era Warrington bought a variety of chassis types, including rare Bristols and Fodens, as well as more typical Guys and Leylands; many had East Lancs bodies. It then moved on to Daimler Fleetlines and, later, Leyland Atlanteans, followed by Dennis Dominators and Leyland Olympians, all with East Lancs bodies. Like many municipalities it also bought rear-engined single-deckers - Bristol RESLs with East Lancs and Seddon bodies.

In the years following deregulation Warrington bought smaller single-deckers - Dodge and later Optare MetroRider minibuses and Dennis Dart midibuses - as well as second-hand buses, including Atlanteans, Dominators, Fleetlines and Olympians, many from other municipal fleets like Derby, Eastbourne, Leicester and Preston.

The current fleet of 115 buses is mainly single-deck, comprising 29 Dennis Darts with Marshall or MCV bodywork, 48 Volvo-badged DAFSB120/Wrights, six Optare Solos and 12 Volvo B7RLE/Wrights. Double-deckers are all second-hand purchases - Leyland Olympians, from Huntingdon & District and Dublin Bus, and Volvo B7TLs from London Central.

The Network Warrington routes serve the town and also reach the neighbouring towns of Altrincham, Leigh and Northwich.

ABOVE Warrington built up a significant fleet of East Lancs-bodied Leyland Atlanteans in the late 1970s and early 1980s; this 1978 AN68A/1R had a 76-seat body and was photographed in 1984. Gavin Booth

BELOW In 2008 Warrington bought 11 ex-Dublin Bus Leyland Olympians with Alexander (Belfast) bodies, dating from 1996. Mark Bailey

Warrington's Merits

Like many municipal operators Warrington moved from a predominantly double-deck fleet to a largely single-deck one from the 1990s, taking regular batches of Dennis Darts, followed from 2003 by several batches of Volvo/Wright Cadets. In the absence of its own midi-size chassis following the withdrawal of the B6BLE from the model lists, Volvo offered the Merit, which was a rebadged DAF/VDL SB120 with Wright bodywork; as a VDL-badged product this body was dubbed Cadet.

A 2007 DAF SB120/Wright Cadet masquerading as a Volvo Merit in the Network Warrington fleet. Paul Godding

LEFT Warrington moved to full-size single-deckers in 2009 when it bought 12 Volvo B7RLEs with Wright Eclipse Urban bodies. Mark Bailey

LEFT In 2011 Warrington bought six of these Optare Solo 25-seaters. Mark Bailey

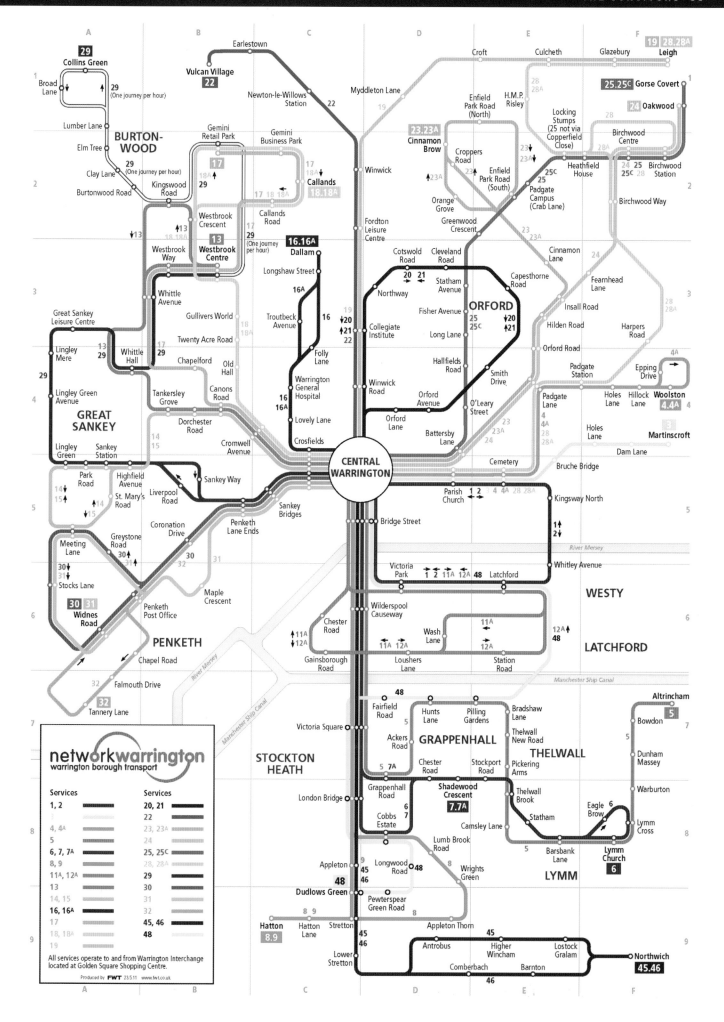

Reading

Local transport in Reading followed the familiar pattern of a horse-tram company bought out by the Corporation (in 1901), electrification (1903) and introduction of motor buses (1919), but the trams were replaced between 1936 and 1939 with trolleybuses, and these last operated in 1968, one of the UK's last systems.

For its motor-bus and trolleybus fleets Reading Corporation Transport for many years bought AECs, most with Park Royal bodies, although it turned to Burlingham to body its final batch of trolleybuses and for AEC Reliance single-deck bus chassis. In the 1970s it bought 'jumbo' Bristol VRTs with Northern Counties bodies, as well as Scania/MCW Metropolitans and MCW Metrobuses and Leyland Titans, being the only municipal customer for this advanced model.

Like many fleets Reading bought many second-hand buses in the years following deregulation, including Volkswagen/Optare minibuses and Volvo-re-engined Leyland Nationals from a number of sources. It went on to buy large numbers of new Optare products, including DAF-based Deltas and Spectras and MAN-based Vectas, as well as integral MetroRiders and Excels.

Optare products were favoured for many years, but in 2012 the 150-strong Reading fleet is dominated by single- and double-deck Scanias; there are integral OmniCity single-deckers and double-deckers, as well as Wright Solar-bodied K230UB single-deckers and East Lancs-bodied double-deckers – N94UD-based OmniDekkas, and N230UDs with the later Olympus body. For a time Reading favoured larger-capacity double-deckers, and some of its OmniDekkas are 90-seaters.

Recent double-deck purchases have included Alexander Dennis Enviro400H hybrid double-deckers and some of the first Wright StreetLite WFs. With 31 diesel-electric hybrids, Reading Buses claimed to have the highest proportion of electric hybrid double-deck buses in its fleet in the UK – one-third of the double-deck fleet. Some are used on the town's busiest route, the 17, which brought electric power back to the Oxford and Wokingham roads for the first time since the trolleybuses were withdrawn.

Reading Buses is a firm adherent of route branding, applying different colours to distinguish the town's 'Premier' routes. There is also the out-of-town route to Newbury, branded 'Jet Black' and operated by local independent Weavaway, under a franchise agreement.

Reading's alternative fuels

In 2008, as bus operators were becoming more interested in alternatives to diesel fuel, Reading Buses introduced 14 Scania OmniCity double-deckers, running on bio-ethanol fuel it believed was made from sugar beet grown in Norfolk but which was, in fact, made from wood pulp imported from Sweden. The buses were converted to run on standard diesel fuel in 2009, and since then Reading has invested heavily in diesel-electric hybrid double-deckers from Alexander Dennis.

One of the 14 bio-ethanol-fuelled Scania OmniCity 77-seat double-deckers bought by Reading Buses in 2008 for the busy 24-hour 17 route, proclaiming its green credentials on the side. Russell Young

LEFT In Reading Buses' generic silver livery, one of the 90-seat Scania N94UD/ East Lancs OmniDekkas bought in 2004, here in use on one of the routes serving the university. Mark Lyons

LEFT 'Bronze 11' branding on a 2006 Reading Buses Scania L94UB with 43-seat Wright Solar body. Mark Lyons

LEFT Reading Buses has invested in Alexander Dennis Enviro400H diesel-electric hybrid double-deckers, and this 2011 78-seater is liveried for the 17 route, on which the type replaced the bio-ethanol Scanias. *Mark Lyons*

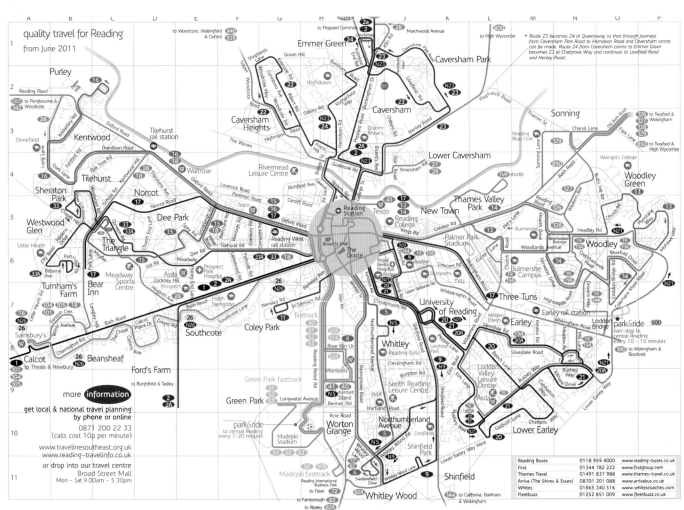

Blackpool

In 2012 Blackpool Transport relaunched its historic tramway with 16 new Bombardier Flexity 2 trams running over track that had been largely replaced. The first electric street tramway in Britain when it opened in 1885, it was taken over by Blackpool Corporation in 1892. Unlike Britain's other traditional tramways, the last of which closed in the 1950s and 1960s, Blackpool continued to operate trams and has done so more or less continuously for 120 years. It started running motor buses in 1921, but not until the 1930s did the bus fleet begin growing in earnest.

In 1986 the arm's-length company Blackpool Transport Services Ltd was set up, and in 1994 this took over the neighbouring Fylde Borough Transport Ltd, which had been bought by its employees the previous year.

The fleet was dominated by Leyland Titans for many years, with Metro-Cammell or locally built Burlingham bodies, but in the 1970s Blackpool turned to single-deckers, a large fleet of Marshall-bodied AEC Swifts being followed in the 1980s by smaller batches of Dennis Lancets and Leyland Nationals, the latter including second-hand examples. Also in the 1980s it bought ex-London Routemasters for its seafront services.

Like a number of other municipal fleets, Blackpool turned to Optare products in the 1980s and 1990s, taking substantial numbers of the Volkswagen-based CityPacer, the DAF-based Delta and the integral Excel and Solo models.

The Fylde takeover in 1994 increased the fleet by 86 buses, of which more than 30 had been bought second-hand by Fylde; these included four Leyland Atlantean chassis that had been rebodied by Northern Counties as single-deckers.

The 2012 fleet still includes a number of Optare products, including Excels and Solos, along with Volvo B7RLEs with Wright or Plaxton bodywork. The double-deck fleet consists of Leyland and Volvo Olympians, including some acquired second-hand, and East Lancs-bodied Dennis Tridents, these also including second-hand examples.

Whilst the tramway has been reopened between Starr Gate and Fleetwood, the bus network also serves the long coastal route as well as the inland part of the town, and into St Annes and Lytham.

ABOVE In the 1960s Blackpool built up a large fleet of Leyland Titan PD3A/1s with 71-seat Metro-Cammell bodies; this one, pictured in 1993, was new in 1967. It is being followed by two East Lancs-bodied Leyland Atlantean AN68A/2Rs dating from 1978. Gavin Booth

BELOW Acquired from Lancashire United in 2007, a 2002 Dennis Trident with 90-seat East Lancs Myllennium Lolyne body still wears the former colour-coded 'Metro Coastlines' livery, with route branding removed and the new Blackpool Transport fleetname added. Mark Lyons

Blackpool's Optares
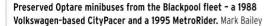

Optare emerged from Leyland Bus's former Roe coachworks in Leeds in 1985. From the start it produced attractively distinctive buses, and it moved quickly from being merely a bodybuilder to become a builder of complete buses. Along the way it offered complete vehicles based on proprietary chassis.

Many municipal fleets have bought Optare products, and Blackpool was an early customer, in 1987/8 buying examples of the CityPacer minibus, based on the Volkswagen LT55 chassis. It then bought DAF SB220-based Deltas before moving on to complete Optare products – MetroRiders, Excels and, more recently, a large fleet of Solos.

Preserved Optare minibuses from the Blackpool fleet – a 1988 Volkswagen-based CityPacer and a 1995 MetroRider. Mark Bailey

LEFT In 2010 Blackpool Transport took delivery of nine 44-seat Plaxton Centro-bodied Volvo B7RLEs painted in the new yellow/black livery. Mark Lyons

LEFT In 2012 Blackpool's the famous coastal tramway was reopened, and 16 new Bombardier Flexity 2 trams were introduced. Mark Bailey

BLACKPOOL TRANSPORT

The tramway between Starr gate and Fleetwood will re-open from Tuesday 3rd April 2012

Copse Road

Knott End Ferry
2C

Fleetwood Ferry

Rossall School
1

T 14

Thornton Gate
4 Cleveleys Park

Cala Gran

Freeport
1

Preesall

Stalmine

3 7

Victoria Road
4

9 16

Cleveleys

16

Four Lane Ends

Hambleton

Anchorsholme Lane
9

Little Bispham
4

Norbreck Shops
7

B&TF College
7

Norcross Roundabout

2c

Norbreck

Bispham Roundabout
3

Kincraig Road

Faraday Way

Rington

Shard Lane Corner

Bispham

Bispham Hotel
3

16

Moor Park

Castle Gardens
14

Poulton
2 15

Cabin

Warbreck

Plymouth Rd Rnd'bt

Little Carleton
2c Blackpool Old Road

15

Empress Drive

Collegiate

2c

Grange Park
11

Gynn Square

Egerton Square

Layton Windmill
9

Grange Road

Staining Road End
2c

Highcross

2

Imperial Hotel
3

North Pier
7

Layton Square
5

16

Normoss Farm

Caunce Street
14

Newton Hall Camp

2 2C 9

BLACKPOOL TOWN CENTRE

Devonshire Square
11

15

Victoria Hospital
5

Plough

Staining
Bibby Drive
15

10 16 17

Central Pier
10

Grasmere Road

Blenheim Road
3

Saddle
16

Worcester Road

Kipling Drive
4

Langdale Road Shops

Central Drive
5

Laurel Avenue

16

Rigby Road/ The Manchester

Lytham Road
11

Ansdell Road
17

Oxford Square

Mereside
Tesco
3 4

South Pier

Waterloo Hotel

14

Spen Corner
3

14

Pleasure Beach & Sandcastle
16

Royal Oak
5

Watson Road

10

Vicarage Lane

ASDA
16

Harrowside

Bond Street

Fishers Field

Highfield Hotel

Midgeland Road
10

Farmers Arms
11

5

Halfway House
7

School Road

Common Edge Road

Starr Gate
1 T

Airport

Spring Gardens
17

Thursby Home

Heeley Road

Heyhouses

Mythop Road
7 11

Saltcotes

17 St Annes Square

St Davids Road

Common Side

Church Road

Lytham Square

St Albans Road

Lindsay Avenue

Ansdell Library
11

Lytham Hospital

Osbourne Road

Fairhaven

Ansdell Footbridge

York Road

Clifton Hospital

www.blackpooltransport.com

LEFT In the 1970s Cardiff switched from a maroon/cream livery to orange/white, as worn by this 1966 Guy Arab V with 65-seat Alexander body. Dale Tringham

FACING PAGE A type rare in municipal service is the TransBus (Dennis/Alexander) Enviro300; this 43-seat example wears the current Cardiff Bus livery. Mark Bailey

Cardiff Bus Managing Director David Brown said: 'Following 100 years of ownership by the city, we are proud to be recognised as one of the leading and best UK bus companies, and these benefits must not be put at risk. We have, however, always recognised that a successful future depends on partnership working. We note the council, at this stage, has stated this is a proposal for discussion only, and as such no commitments have been made. We need to ensure any changes are in the best interests of our customers, our staff and the city as a whole.'

In the event, nothing happened.

Cardiff

Cardiff Corporation took over a private horse-tramway company in 1902 and proceeded to electrify the system; the trams were replaced by trolleybuses between 1942 and 1950, and the last trolleybus ran in 1970.

Motor buses had been bought from 1920, and although AECs were favoured for many years, in the post-war era Cardiff bought a more varied selection of bus types. In the 1950s the fleet also included Bristols, Crossleys, Daimlers and Guys, many with bodies by local builders Bruce, D. J. Davies and Longwell Green, although East Lancs products appeared in the late 1950s.

Later Cardiff bought Bristol VRTs, Daimler Fleetlines and Volvo Ailsas, as well as MCW and Optare Metroriders, Leyland Lynxes and Olympians, and Scania N113 single- and double-deckers. It later bought second-hand Ailsas from Merseyside and Fife Scottish, and the Ailsas outlived other double-deckers in the fleet.

Today Cardiff's 230-strong bus fleet is largely single-deck, ranging from a large battalion of Pointer Darts – representing two-thirds of the fleet – to articulated and rigid Scania OmniCity and Scania/ Wrights, as well as Alexander Dennis Enviro300s. There are also 14 Scania N270/East Lancs Olympus double-deckers.

In 2007 there were suggestions that Cardiff Council might sell up to 40% of Cardiff Bus as part of a package to bring in additional funding. The council's Chief Executive, Byron Davies, said: 'We have been looking at the possibility of a potential partner for Cardiff Bus but with the council retaining majority control. We would expect our partners to grow the existing business and provide an even better service for the people of Cardiff. It would be in their interests to do so.'

Cardiff's Ailsas

Standardisation was perhaps less important to Cardiff Bus between the 1970s and 1990s than ensuring that it had a good flow of new buses to put on the road. In these years it bought, for its double-deck fleet, Bristol VRTs with Alexander bodies, Volvo Ailsas with Northern Counties bodies, Leyland Olympians with East Lancs bodies and Scania N113s with Alexander bodies.

The front-engined Ailsas were an interesting choice for a municipal fleet; Tayside bought substantial batches, and Derby took 15, while Cardiff received 36 with Northern Counties bodies in the years 1982-4. Cardiff even went on to acquire second-hand examples, between 1996 and 1999 buying 12 that had been new to Merseyside PTE and eight that had started life with Fife Scottish; all of these had Alexander bodies.

The Ailsas outlived the other double-deck types bought at the time and continued in service until the end of 2007, being often pressed into service on peak-hour relief duties.

One of Cardiff's own Northern Counties-bodied Volvo Ailsas, new in 1982, is pursued by a 1984 Alexander-bodied Ailsa acquired in 1999 from Fife Scottish. Note the Welsh-language Bws Caerdydd fleetname. Paul Godding

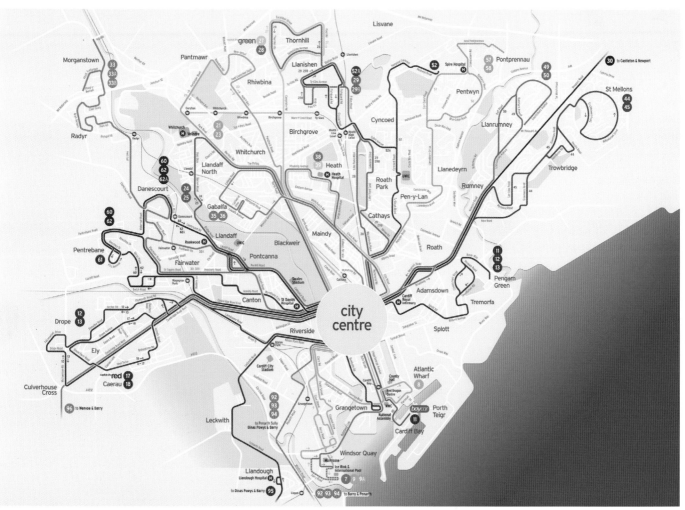

ABOVE A 2006 Cardiff Bus Scania OmniCity 53-seat artic liveried for the 'Baycar' service linking the city with the growing Bay area. Russell Young

RIGHT Cardiff's first new double-deckers for more than a decade were 14 Scania N270UDs with 74-seat East Lancs Olympus bodies, delivered in 2007. Mark Bailey

Nottingham

By far the largest of the surviving English municipal bus companies is Nottingham City Transport, with a fleet of some 350 buses. It serves an historic city at the heart of a substantial urban area with a population of around 670,000.

Nottingham Corporation bought a private horse-tram operator in 1897 and quickly electrified and expanded the system. Motor buses first appeared in 1906, but serious bus operation started in the 1920s. Trolleybuses were used to replace the trams between 1927 and 1936 and survived until 1966.

In 1968 Nottingham City Transport (as it was now known) acquired the neighbouring West Bridgford UDC bus undertaking. Nottingham City Transport Ltd (NCT) was set up in 1986 as an arm's-length company, and in 1992 it acquired the independent South Notts company.

The motor-bus fleet was always a mixed one, and in the 1970s and 1980s Nottingham bought a range of double-deck types – rear-engined Atlanteans, Fleetlines and Scanias and underfloor-engined Leyland Lions and Volvo Citybuses, later adding Leyland and Volvo Olympians as well as rare Dennis Arrows. The current fleet is largely standardised on Optare and Scania products, the former including Optare Solos and Versas, the latter substantial numbers of integral CN94 OmniCity single-deckers (plus some N94/East Lancs OmniTowns and Wright-bodied L94 artics) and N94- and N270-based OmniDekkas.

Nottingham's present-day network provides comprehensive coverage of the city as well as routes beyond its boundaries, to Loughborough and Southwell. In 2001 NCT launched its 'Go2' and

'Network' brands; Go2 routes operate a 10-minute daytime frequency, and the buses carry a range of colours to help passengers identify their routes.

In 2004 trams returned to Nottingham. NET (Nottingham Express Transit) was operated by Arrow Light Rail, a consortium that included NCT and Transdev, the French multinational transport operator, which had acquired an effective 18% stake in NCT in 2000. Phase 2 of the tramway is under construction, though this will be built and operated by Nottingham Tramlink, a consortium including Wellglade, which group's Trent Barton subsidiary is the other major bus operator in the city.

ABOVE Crossing the city-centre tramlines, a 2004 Scania CN94UB OmniCity in Citylink Park & Ride colours. Mark Bailey

LEFT Representing Nottingham's preference for big double-deckers, a long-wheelbase Scania N94UD/ East Lancs OmniDekka 87-seater in Go2 'Pink Line' livery. Paul Godding

FACING PAGE ABOVE Seen at Nottingham railway station on the Unilink service, a Scania L94UA with Wright Solar Fusion body. Mark Bailey

FACING PAGE BELOW Nottingham returned to trams in 2004 after nearly 70 years, and Nottingham City Transport was involved in the consortium that opened the new tramway. This is one of the 15 Derby-built Bombardier Incentro trams that formed the original fleet. All are named; this is William Booth, recalling the founder ofthe Salvation Army, who was born in Nottingham. Mark Bailey

ABOVE A 2008 Optare Versa in use on the Pathfinder service that links Nottingham with the pretty town of Southwell, beyond the city boundary. Mark Bailey

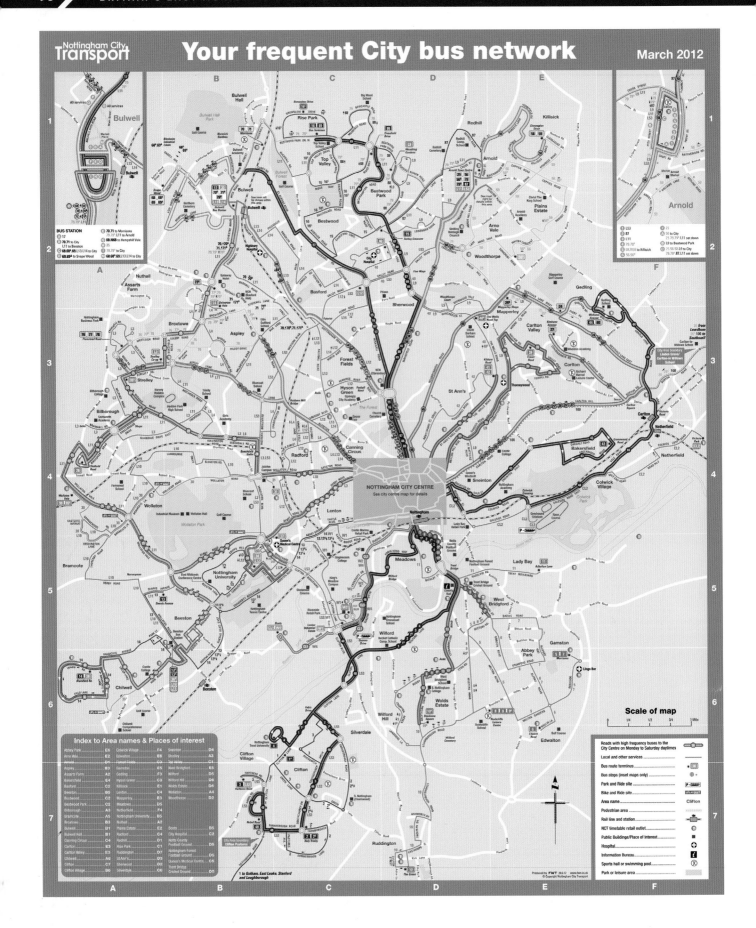

Nottingham City Transport

Your frequent City bus network

March 2012

Nottingham's distinctive buses

For many years the larger municipal operators were able to specify bus bodies that were designed to their own individual specifications, and it was possible to identify 'Birmingham' or 'Manchester' buses by their looks. However, as bodybuilders concentrated on more standardised products, buses were built to a smaller range of designs.

One operator that bucked the trend was Nottingham, which from the 1960s received many batches of rear-engined (and,

later, underfloor-engined) double-deckers with bodies to a distinctly 'Nottingham' style. These were dual-door, with a narrow entrance by the driver, and were configured internally to achieve maximum seating capacity, with seats in some unusual positions. Thus Nottingham managed to fit 78 seats in standard-length dual-door buses and 80 seats (and more) in some. With the advent of low-floor double-deckers Nottingham has bought buses to standard body styles but to 12m length, with seats for 90 passengers and more.

LEFT This 1997 nearside view of a 1981 Leyland Atlantean AN68C/1R reveals the narrow front doorway. The 78-seat body was by Northern Counties. Tony Wilson

BELOW Various builders produced bodywork to Nottingham's distinctive style. Pictured in 1978, this 1973 Leyland Atlantean AN68/1R had a 77-seat East Lancs body. Gavin Booth

Lothian

Lothian Buses is by far the largest of the 11 municipal bus companies surviving in 2012, with around 650 buses for its service network plus another 50 for its significant tours operation in the Scottish capital.

Edinburgh Corporation began direct operations of its transport department in 1919, assuming control of the cable tramway and buying its first motor buses for regular service work. In 1920 the neighbouring burgh of Leith was taken over by Edinburgh, and the Leith electric trams passed into Edinburgh Corporation control. The Edinburgh cable system was increasingly troublesome, so the city tramways were electrified in 1922, allowing through running to Leith and to Musselburgh and Port Seton in the east. The bus fleet grew in the 1920s and 1930s, augmenting the tramway network, but from the early 1950s the trams were replaced by buses, with the conversion completed in 1956. In 1975 Lothian Region Transport took over the Edinburgh Corporation buses, and in 2000 the company was renamed Lothian Buses.

The first buses were Leylands and AECs, but from the mid-1930s Edinburgh favoured Daimlers, then Leylands from the early 1950s, amassing substantial fleets of Titans and Atlanteans. Lothian turned to Leyland and later Volvo Olympians, then Dennis Tridents and Volvo B7TLs and B9TLs. For many years it favoured Alexander bodies, switching to Plaxton for the Tridents and Wright for the low-floor Volvos. The single-deck fleet has grown in recent years, first with Dennis/Plaxton SPD Darts and later with Wright-bodied Volvo B7RLEs.

From the very start Edinburgh Corporation bought charabancs for city tours, and Edinburgh and Lothian have continued to provide tours in the city. In recent years the tour business has been built up, and Lothian now offers a range of different tour brands using a fleet of open-top and semi-open-top Dennis Tridents and former London Routemasters.

Although Edinburgh routes were largely confined to the city boundaries, from 1986 Lothian expanded into the areas around Edinburgh, most successfully into East Lothian and Midlothian, where it has become the major operator of high-frequency routes into Edinburgh.

In 2011 Lothian bought 15 Alexander Dennis Enviro400H diesel-electric hybrid double-deckers and has shown a close interest in alternatives to diesel fuel.

Lothian's big buses

A high seating capacity has long been important to Lothian Buses and its predecessor, Edinburgh Corporation. Its tram-replacement buses were 60-63-seaters, and its first rear-engined buses were 75-seat Leyland Atlanteans. When it moved on to Leyland Olympians it chose 33ft-long buses with up to 83 seats, and when it sought low-floor double-deckers it chose extra-long Dennis Tridents and Volvo B7TLs and B9TLs with seating for up to 83 passengers.

Lothian's standard double-deckers since the mid-2000s have been extra-long Volvo/Wrights; this is a 2009 B9TL 78-seater, with branding for the busy 22 route. Gavin Booth

ABOVE In recent years Lothian has reverted to a more traditional livery layout, using a version of the maroon/white colours that have been worn by Edinburgh's buses since 1919. This is a 2011 delivery, a 79-seat Volvo B9TL/Wright Eclipse Gemini. Gavin Booth

FACING PAGE TOP Lothian Buses bought Dennis/Plaxton SPD Darts like this 2003 42-seater, seen in 2010. Gavin Booth

FACING PAGE BOTTOM Subsequent Lothian single-deckers were Wright Eclipse Urban-bodied Volvo B7RLEs; this 2007 37-seater displays the original branding for the 29 route. Gavin Booth

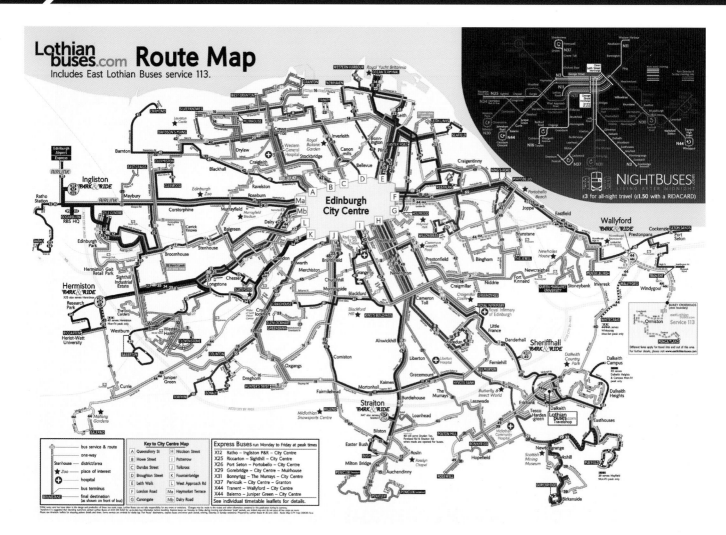

ABOVE Most of the buses in Lothian's tour fleet are older low-floor double-deckers converted from conventional buses. This is one of five Dennis Trident/Alexander ALX400s supplied in 1999, now in 71-seat semi-open-top form and in 'City Sightseeing' livery. Gavin Booth

RIGHT Lothian's Mac Tours operation employs ex-London Routemasters, including 10 extra-long ERM types; this one was new in 1959. Gavin Booth

FACING PAGE Lothian Buses has shown interest in hybrid and gas buses and in 2011 bought 15 ADL Enviro400H hybrids. Gavin Booth

Epilogue
IN PRAISE OF MUNICIPAL BUSES

ABOVE Lothian's branded buses display local place names and historical references; this 2007 Volvo B7TL/ Wright Eclipse Gemini 81-seater is in the new standard livery with a turquoise top for the 37/47 routes to Penicuik, in Midlothian. Gavin Booth

For many of Britain's towns and cities it was a badge of honour to field a fleet of trams, trolleybuses and motor buses in the civic colours, proudly displaying the civic coat of arms, and – lest the symbolism be lost on anyone – they often bore the name of the town, sometimes in splendidly ornate shaded lettering. They would look with sympathy at those towns served by buses that bore only the name of some regional giant.

Municipal transport was not just a matter of civic pride, however. It was the way that many towns grew, allowing the townspeople to get to work, to school, to the shops, to the cinema, and allowing them to live further from the often overcrowded town centres, in the suburbs that grew up around the tramlines and the bus routes. It was a public service, and, while the trams and buses were never expected to make huge profits, it was important that they make some sort of contribution to the public purse. And they usually did.

The municipal transport manager, whose name often appeared on the side of the local buses, was an important official, though he – inevitably he – had to go cap-in-hand to the transport committee to ask for money to buy new buses, or improve his garage facilities. Some managers developed good relationships with the councillors and usually got what they wanted, while others had to toe the line of whichever political party was in power.

The fact that 91 bus operators survived in municipal hands until 1968 testifies to the local importance of the services provided. But things started to change

from 1969, when all municipalities in the seven largest British conurbations outside London were swept up into the brave new world of the Passenger Transport Executive. Of the rest, West Bridgford passed to neighbouring Nottingham in 1968, the same year Haslingden and Rawtenstall formed Rossendale; Exeter and Luton passed to the new National Bus Company in 1970, and numbers were reduced by a further four by local-government reorganisation in 1974, when Darwen passed to Blackburn, Morecambe & Heysham to Lancaster, and Bedwas & Machen, Caerphilly and Gelligaer were reformed as Rhymney Valley. In 1977 Waveney closed down.

The 46 that were left stood firm until the uncertainties of deregulation came along to unsettle the *status quo*. For the first time in recent memory, municipal bus services were not protected by the route-licensing system that emerged from the 1930 Road Traffic Act. Like all British bus operators outside London they faced possible competition from local National Bus Company or Scottish Bus Group fleets, from existing independent operators or from the rash of new smaller operators that emerged to take advantage of the new freedoms.

Some municipals realised that they were in a fortunate position. While other operators would need buses, staff and premises to compete in urban centres, the incumbent operators could expand beyond their normal operating area – often the town boundaries – by using just a few additional buses on an extended existing route.

BELOW Big, brightly coloured, branded buses are a recurring theme among the remaining municipal bus fleets. Reading Buses has moved to colour-coded routes; seen on one of its 'Pink Routes' is a 2008 Scania OmniCity 77-seater, one of the buses that previously ran on bio-ethanol. Mark Lyons

FACING PAGE TOP Blackpool has moved away from its Metro Coastlines image, as seen on this ex-Lancashire United Dennis Trident/East Lancs Myllennium Lolyne 90-seater. Mark Lyons

FACING PAGE BOTTOM Buses on Nottingham's high-frequency Go2 routes wear a range of colour schemes. This 2011 Scania/ Optare OmniDekka is on the 'Yellow Line' 68, a fact echoed in the front destination display. Mark Bailey

ABOVE Although Cardiff has a standard fleet livery, its Scania OmniCity artics wear distinctive brands, like 'Cardiff City Red'. Mark Lyons

Some tackled competition better than others, and while Reading and Southend famously decided to start operating express services into London, and Maidstone decided to have a go at London tendering – successfully, at least in terms of winning contracts – most recognised that their strength lay in their local knowledge and, indeed, local loyalties, and promoted day and weekly tickets to build on these. Others, however, decided that the income from the sale of their transport undertakings could yield much-needed cash, and from 1988 the process of sell-offs started, while a few simply perished along the way. Between then and 1992 the total number of municipals dropped by 13, and 1993 turned out to be the busiest year of all, 12 municipalities selling their arm's-length companies. Thereafter the process slowed, leaving us with just 11 municipal bus companies.

Those that are left have tended to protect their territory by providing good-quality bus services using increasingly better vehicles. Unlike the mega-groups, whose local managers are often under pressure from their corporate bosses to achieve profit percentages in double figures, municipal companies are able to feed profits back into the company, while paying a modest dividend to their local-authority shareholders.

This has meant that the municipals often plough a different furrow from that of the big groups. Large double-deckers seating up to 90 passengers have been popular with Lothian, Nottingham and Reading, for instance, and without the shackles of corporate liveries several have gone firmly down the route branding avenue, some opting for coloured tops, and others – notably Nottingham and Reading – going for different strong colours to help passengers distinguish their buses.

Local control also means that municipal buses are not managed from some distant centre; as a result, managers are more aware of what is happening on their patch and can ensure that standards of vehicle and staff presentation do not drop.

Nobody can forecast how long the 11 surviving municipal bus companies will remain in local ownership, but among them are companies that constantly pick up important transport awards and are often judged to be among the best bus companies in Britain. As we have seen, passengers and other locals can get very heated at any threat to remove their buses from civic ownership, which is surely testimony to the fine service that local people have enjoyed, often for more than a century.

Appendix
MUNICIPAL OPERATORS AND THEIR FLEETS

ABOVE The Wrightbus StreetLite WF in 2012 – a new type of bus for a municipal company.
This is one of six delivered to Reading Buses to replace Optare Solos. Mark Lyons

*Including trams
+Including trolleybuses
++Trolleybuses only

1938

Aberdare	26
Aberdeen	213 *
Accrington	50
Ashton-under-Lyne	52 *+
Barrow-in-Furness	50
Bedwas & Machen	3
Birkenhead	158
Birmingham	1,563 *+
Blackburn	101 *
Blackpool	377 *
Bolton	223 *
Bournemouth	173 +
Bradford	348 *+
Brighton	80 **
Burnley, Colne & Nelson	137
Burton-upon-Trent	41
Bury	104
Caerphilly	16
Cardiff	268 *
Chester	28
Chesterfield	85 +
Cleethorpes	36 +
Colchester	29
Coventry	162 *
Darlington	43 ++
Darwen	37 *
Derby	117 +
Doncaster	80 +
Dundee	148 *
Eastbourne	50
Edinburgh	553 *
Exeter	54
Gelligaer	14
Glasgow	1,625 *
Great Yarmouth	44
Grimsby	57 +
Halifax	172 *
Haslingden	15
Huddersfield	233 *+
Ipswich	68 ++
Kingston-upon-Hull	271 *+
Lancaster	27
Leeds	669
Leicester	271 *
Leigh	38
Lincoln	44
Liverpool	860 *
Lowestoft	17
Luton	63
Lytham St Annes	40
Maidstone	33 +
Manchester	1,272 *
Merthyr Tydfil	23
Middlesbrough	46
Morecambe & Heysham	44
Newcastle	395 *+
Newport	74
Northampton	79
Nottingham	310 +
Oldham	204 *
Plymouth	206 *
Pontypridd	28 +
Portsmouth	237 +
Preston	74
Ramsbottom	15
Rawtenstall	45
Reading	85 *+

Rochdale	116
Rotherham	125 *+
St Helens	75 +
Salford	316 *
Sheffield	739 *
South Shields	58 *+
Southampton	171 *
Southend	84 *+
Southport	54
SHMD Board	85 *
Stockport	170 *
Stockton	59
Sunderland	122 *
Swindon	41
Tees-side Railless TB	19 +
Todmorden	38
Wallasey	96
Walsall	167 +
Warrington	58
West Bridgford	23
West Bromwich	53
West Hartlepool	46 +
West Mon Board	17
Widnes	21
Wigan	94
Wolverhampton	178 +

1952

Aberdare	45
Aberdeen	269 *
Accrington	60
Ashton-under-Lyne	74 +
Barrow-in-Furness	73
Bedwas & Machen	4
Birkenhead	223
Birmingham	1,919 *+
Blackburn	111
Blackpool	375 *
Bolton	285
Bournemouth	206 +
Bradford	368 +
Brighton	87 +
Burnley, Colne & Nelson	161
Burton-upon-Trent	52
Bury	104
Caerphilly	15
Cardiff	240 +
Chester	48
Chesterfield	135
Cleethorpes	35 +
Colchester	35
Coventry	314
Darlington	69 +
Darwen	35
Derby	162 +
Doncaster	111 +
Dundee	209 *
Eastbourne	58
Edinburgh	699 *
Exeter	85
Gelligaer	26
Glasgow	2,047 *+
Great Yarmouth	53
Grimsby	74 +
Halifax	170
Haslingden	17
Huddersfield	228 +

Ipswich	83 +
Kingston-upon-Hull	252 +
Lancaster	46
Leeds	785 *
Leicester	236
Leigh	65
Lincoln	58
Liverpool	1,117 *
Llandudno	15
Lowestoft	17
Luton	63
Lytham St Annes	45
Maidstone	42 +
Manchester	1,533 +
Merthyr Tydfil	67
Middlesbrough	74
Morecambe & Heysham	56
Newcastle	465 +
Newport	123
Northampton	92
Nottingham	423 +
Oldham	240
Plymouth	288
Pontypridd	60 +
Portsmouth	254 +
Preston	103
Ramsbottom	19
Rawtenstall	54
Reading	104 +
Rochdale	156
Rotherham	154 +
St Helens	155 +
Salford	324
Sheffield	991 *
South Shields	93 +
Southampton	195
Southend	82 +
Southport	84
SHMD Board	81
Stockport	168
Stockton	101
Sunderland	210 *
Swindon	55
Tees-side Railless TB	41 +
Todmorden	40
Wallasey	108
Walsall	245 +
Warrington	91
West Bridgford	24
West Bromwich	112
West Hartlepool	55
West Mon	30
Widnes	40
Wigan	162
Wolverhampton	298 +

1959

Aberdare	43
Aberdeen	236
Accrington	59
Ashton-under-Lyne	68 +
Barrow-in-Furness	63
Bedwas & Machen	7
Birkenhead	225
Birmingham	1,823
Blackburn	109
Blackpool	324 *

Bolton	279
Bournemouth	179 +
Bradford	388 +
Brighton	70 +
Burnley, Colne & Nelson	147
Burton-upon-Trent	45
Bury	98
Caerphilly	30
Cardiff	277 +
Chester	50
Chesterfield	130
Colchester	38
Colwyn Bay	5
Coventry	309
Darlington	63
Darwen	34
Derby	165 +
Doncaster	111 +
Dundee	240
Eastbourne	54
Edinburgh	713
Exeter	65
Gelligaer	28
Glasgow	1,918 *+
Great Yarmouth	63
Grimsby-Cleethorpes	99 +
Halifax	165
Hartlepool	4
Haslingden	18
Huddersfield	218 +
Ipswich	72 +
Kingston-upon-Hull	239 +
Lancaster	36
Leeds	690 *
Leicester	215
Leigh	61
Lincoln	57
Liverpool	1,245
Llandudno	17
Lowestoft	17
Luton	65
Lytham St Annes	42
Maidstone	44 +
Manchester	1,448 +
Merthyr Tydfil	74
Middlesbrough	90
Morecambe & Heysham	54
Newcastle	433 +
Newport	115
Northampton	91
Nottingham	447 +
Oldham	235
Plymouth	273
Pontypridd	53
Portsmouth	234 +
Preston	100
Ramsbottom	18
Rawtenstall	51
Reading	113 +
Rochdale	151
Rotherham	141 +
St Helens	145 +
Salford	324
Sheffield	946 *
South Shields	100 +
Southampton	186
Southend	84
Southport	73
SHMD Board	84
Stockport	168
Stockton	100
Sunderland	185
Swindon	66

Tees-side Railless TB	41 +
Todmorden	40
Wallasey	104
Walsall	253 +
Warrington	141
West Bridgford	28
West Bromwich	117
West Hartlepool	63
West Mon Board	30
Widnes	40
Wigan	154
Wolverhampton	296 +

1976

Aberconwy	10
Barrow-in-Furness	67
Blackburn	135
Blackpool	243 *
Bournemouth	159
Brighton	64
Burnley & Pendle	128
Cardiff	210
Chester	51
Chesterfield	137
Cleveland	309
Colchester	53
Colwyn Bay	3
Cynon Valley	38
Darlington	70
Derby	168
Eastbourne	64
East Staffordshire	40
Fylde	39
Grampian	236
Great Yarmouth	64
Grimsby-Cleethorpes	98
Halton	42
Hartlepool	92
Hyndburn	55
Ipswich	78
Islwyn	30
Kingston-upon-Hull	240
Lancaster	97
Leicester	231
Lincoln	61
Lothian	686
Maidstone	47
Merthyr Tydfil	80
Newport	107
Northampton	78
Nottingham	476
Plymouth	216
Portsmouth	179
Preston	97
Reading	131
Rhymney Valley	69
Rossendale	51
Southampton	196
Southend	72
Taff-Ely	42
Tayside	242
Thamesdown	70
Warrington	79
Waveney	20

1991

Blackburn	118
Blackpool	211 *
Bournemouth	124
Brighton	78
Burnley & Pendle	101

Cardiff	240
Chester	83
Cleveland	141
Colchester	56
Cynon Valley	39
Darlington	65
Eastbourne	48
Fylde	84
Great Yarmouth	51
Grimsby-Cleethorpes	108
Halton	52
Hartlepool	62
Hyndburn	87
Ipswich	103
Islwyn	41
Kingston-upon-Hull	219
Lancaster	62
Leicester	222
Lincoln	55
Lothian	576
Maidstone	118
Newport	96
Northampton	65
Nottingham	419
Plymouth	178
Preston	140
Reading	140
Rossendale	77
Southampton	155
Southend	95
Tayside	170
Thamesdown	130
Warrington	117

2001

Blackburn	106
Blackpool	257 *
Bournemouth	119
Cardiff	265
Chester	95
Eastbourne	47
Halton	56
Ipswich	88
Islwyn	36
Lothian	511
Newport	85
Nottingham	442
Plymouth	189
Reading	220
Rossendale	100
Thamesdown	120
Warrington	95

2012

Blackpool	159
Cardiff	232
Halton	60
Ipswich	76
Lothian	650
Newport	96
Nottingham	351
Reading	152
Rossendale	90
Thamesdown	90
Warrington	115